Reclaim Your Creative Soul

*The secrets to organizing your full-time life
to make room for your craft*

By Crissi Langwell

This book is also available in ebook.
Please visit the author's website to find out where to
purchase this book.
www.crissilangwell.com

Dedicated to YOU.
May this book help you to feed your creative soul.

Table of Contents

Prologue

Have You Lost Your Creative Edge?

Hey. I'd like to talk with you for a moment. Yes, you, the frustrated artist. And you, the writer with no time to write. And you as well, musicians, visionaries, crafters, and creators. You, the one who is having a difficult time balancing, even merging, your creative life with your everyday life.

You're probably filled with resentment toward anything that stands between you and your creativity. If your art isn't what pays your bills, you likely hate your job. If you are married with kids, you may find yourself wishing your family away—at least for a little while so you can accomplish *anything* creative. Any phone calls you receive, tasks added to your plate, friends who want to hang out, chores that need to be done, bills that need to be paid, errands that need to be run, homework that needs to be checked, dinner that needs to be cooked, dog that needs to be walked…they are all blocking your path toward creativity.

You likely feel overwhelmed by the daily grind, and feel like the mundane is taking over every inspiring part of your life. The stuff you don't want to do is slowly consuming the time you would rather be using on your art, writing, or other creative outlet.

I can bet your frustration is mounting because of this, only adding to the list of creativity blockers. If you can't overcome frustration, your creativity will remain stifled. You'll end up restless, unable to conjure up anything within your craft.

Perhaps you long for those days when creativity was at your fingertips. You probably measure your present life against the life you had back then, when nothing stood in between you and your art.

But now?

There are projects you've started but can't seem to finish. You feel overwhelmed by a ton of ideas but have no time to complete any of them—or the opposite: you can't seem to grasp even one idea. Maybe you are fitting in time to work on your craft, but still feel like you have nothing to show for it. Or maybe you have some finished projects, but know that you are capable of so much more.

Your spirit is crying out to you, begging you to allow it to unleash its creativity. You want to comply, but life keeps getting in the way. You aren't sure how to balance everything you *have* to do with all the things you *want* to do.

You feel unfulfilled and incomplete, watching your life as an artist slip away with each passing breath.

You did not sign up for this life.

Except...you did.

I know. Because this was my life. And if I'm not completely careful, this becomes my life all over again.

My name is Crissi Langwell, and I have been a writer and storyteller for as long as I can remember. I also have a full-time job, a family with three teenagers, I am an active leader in my church, I volunteer in my writing club, and I have managed to write two or more books a year for the past three years.

How is this possible? By dedicating myself to my craft, focusing my intentions, and being diligent in every area of my life.

However, it isn't always easy. Before I share the secrets to reclaim your creativity, let me tell you a story—MY story.

RECLAIM YOUR CREATIVE SOUL

How I Became a Writer

As kids, my sister, Melissa, and I shared a room. Long after we were supposed to be asleep, Melissa and I would lay awake giggling as we whispered secrets to each other. Ultimately, these gab fests would turn into storytelling sessions. My sister would beg me to tell her a story, and I would happily comply by pulling out my flashlight and preparing my shadow puppets (aka, my hands). With my characters in place, I would share the story of Samantha and Mark, a bossy older sister and her annoying little brother. These two siblings would always have some sort of dilemma that needed overcoming, or an issue that was making them feel all the feelings. Ultimately, one of them would do something that pissed off the other and they would end up fighting. Spoiler alert: the story would usually end with one of the shadow puppets getting really, really huge, and then eating their sibling.

Mark and Samantha weren't the only characters whose stories I shared. I spun tales about dragons and princesses in faraway lands, sent us on imagined voyages upon the back of a Pegasus, plunged us into the sea with mermaids and sea folk, battled everyday bullies before flying away like Superman, described secret passageways that led to Eden-like hideaways.... I was a storyteller, and I looked forward to bedtime when I could begin where I left off the night before.

In high school, I enrolled in a creative writing class. Every high school needs to have this class. I had already been entertaining my family for years with gifts of stories for birthdays and Christmases, and I spent as much time writing as I did reading other people's words. So when creative writing was offered as a class at my school, I couldn't wait to enroll. The class stretched my writing abilities, forcing me to write every day instead of just when the mood was right. Sometimes we even shared our work. This was a foreign concept to me, as the only people who ever read my writing were my teachers and my family. But I fought through the shyness, and strengthened my writing through the feedback my classmates gave me. I also learned more about storytelling through the stories of the other people in my class

I was on fire for writing. If it wasn't clear before, it was definitely clear during this high school class—writing was my passion. Somehow, I was going to make writing a huge part of my adult life.

Things turned interesting after high school, however. You see, I was in love. And when you're in love, everything else takes second place. My writing was pushed aside as I reveled in romance and devoted my time to a boy my parents weren't exactly fond of. We moved in together the day after high school. A year later, I was moving back into my parents' house, expecting their first grandchild. A very long story short, I had a baby girl, married the boy my parents didn't like, and then had a baby boy. I picked writing back up again, telling stories about our family with a community of other writers who were doing the same. Back then we called these online diaries. Today, they'd be considered blogs.

My marriage to this boy my parents didn't like ended up being a bit of a nightmare. Following the unfortunate loss of our third child to stillbirth, our terrible marriage took a drastic turn for the worse. I eventually left, thus starting my life as a single mother.

Things got pretty bad before they got better. I spent about a year on my parents' couch, licking my wounds as I mourned my failed marriage. And when I could pull myself together, I began working with my dad as his assistant in his real estate appraising business. However, it was totally the wrong time to enter real estate. The market was tanking, and my dad urged me to find a "real" job.

That's when I found the job at the newspaper.

They were hiring for an advertising assistant in the real estate department. Thanks to this brief job with my dad, I now had a background in real estate. It was as if the stars had aligned to open a door to the job of my dreams. No, not the advertising assistant job, but a job at the newspaper.

The newspaper was a huge part of my growing up years. My dad always woke up early to start reading the paper with a cup of coffee. As an early riser, I'd join him and read the comics. Eventually, I graduated to my own cup of coffee, as well as reading the sections that surrounded the comics. It became our routine. This routine was especially important in my teenage years when we couldn't see eye to eye about anything, but would still show up at the kitchen table just to read the paper together. It was how we connected when we couldn't even look at each other. Those mornings served as mini truces to the war between a rebellious teenage girl and her protective father.

My favorite columnist was Susan Schwartz, a woman who wrote candid articles about growing older, supporting friends through breast cancer, the wonders of a long walk or a good conversation in general, and the benefits of being healthy. She wrote about everyday life—nothing extraordinary, just her normal daily routine. But she wrote about it in a way that made me want to live it right alongside her. And through her column, I did. She invited readers to join her daily journey. Reading her column made me feel like I was talking with a friend.

To work at the newspaper with writers like her would be living my dream. And my dream came true when I was called back for a few more interviews before finally being hired.

Well, it sort of came true.

There are many different working parts at a newspaper to get the news out to people every morning. The two most known parts are the advertising department and the journalism department. A newspaper cannot survive without either one of these departments. The journalists write the news that gets in the hands of the people. And the advertising department sells and creates the ads that pay the bills so that these papers can continue to be produced. These two parts go hand-in-hand. But these two departments do not.

When I first started working at the newspaper, I came in there like a star-struck teenager. I was sure I would see some of my idols in the newsroom. Imagine my surprise when I found out that the advertising department was on a completely different level of the building than the newsroom. Not only did I not see any of my idols, the two departments didn't even speak to each other. It was as if we were working for different companies.

So my job of working at a newspaper was fulfilled, but not in the way I had hoped. The most creative part of my job was when I was able to help build ads for the real estate agents. Occasionally I even got the chance to ghostwrite articles about a listed house or two, which allowed me to pretend I was one of the greats up in the newsroom. It wasn't exactly my dream, and I definitely experienced moments of unrest. *But I worked for the newspaper.*

A couple years in, a new position opened for someone to lay out the newspaper. I applied for the position and got the job. With it came more money and more hours, two things I desperately needed for my single-income family. The kids and I had moved into our own place, and finally we could afford to live there without wondering if we'd have to skip a few meals to pay the bills.

I was still writing about my family, this time from the perspective of a single mother. It eventually included dating as a single parent, as I began seeing one of my coworkers, the man who would eventually become my husband.

Two things happened during this time. First, the publisher of the newspaper discovered my blog, and he liked it. Second, one of my coworkers introduced me to NaNoWriMo, also known as National Novel Writing Month, held in the month of November. In the same period of time, my job set me up with a blog for the newspaper to start writing about my family life, and I began to seriously consider writing my first novel.

By the end of November, I had the first (and only) draft of a poorly written novel. It was so bad, I knew I'd never do anything with it. But having completed it, the possibility of actually writing a book for people to read become a reality. More than that, my blog was taking off. It soon became a regular column in the newspaper and I moved into the newsroom.

Let's pause here and soak that in. I went from a divorced single mom with hardly any significant work experience, to placing ads in the Classifieds section of the newspaper, to now rubbing elbows with the real journalists in the newsroom.

I had made it.

The primary part of my job became running a family website for the newspaper where I connected with a community of other mothers. My duty was to find ways to draw readers in by utilizing a forum, social media, and my blog to gather interest. It was a dream come true. Through this position, I became educated in website management, social media, content producing, and everything else that encompasses the job of an online producer.

I was living my dream. And then, I wasn't.

The family website tanked. There was interest from the community, but not enough to draw in advertisers to support the site. My job would have been in jeopardy, except my boss saw my potential. He handed me the keys to the newspaper's new entertainment website, allowing me to be the manager of that site as well. And while it did really well, it still didn't do well enough. Once again, I was a web producer without a website. I was moved into another new position—this time as the content producer of the whole newspaper website.

Let me tell you what this job entails. Copying and pasting other people's words. There's more, but that was the bulk of it. This mundane job took up so much of my time, the creative part of my job became less and less and less...until the creativity of my job was phased out completely.

Luckily, I was still writing in my spare time—this time, books. My first NaNoWriMo book may have been a total flop, but the second NaNoWriMo, I wrote a story that had real potential. By the time the third NaNo was through, I had a rough draft that I knew was going to be a book. That year I got married to that handsome co-worker I mentioned earlier, and then I wrote the rough draft of my book, *A Symphony of Cicadas*. After a few months of editing, I self-published my very first book in 2013. Following that book, I wrote and released the follow-up, *Forever Thirteen*, as well as a collection of my parenting columns in *Golf Balls, Eight Year Olds & Dual Paned Windows,* and a book of my poetry in *Everything I Am Not Saying.* I joined my local writing chapter, Redwood Writers, and eventually became their newsletter editor. I then released my third fiction book, *The Road to Hope,* written during that second year of NaNoWriMo. And in 2015, I published my fourth fiction novel, *Come Here, Cupcake.*

To say I am busy is an understatement. I still work at the newspaper as their online content producer. Besides that job, I also do freelance editing, formatting, and website development for other authors to help fund my book publishing, and because I love this type of work. I am still the editor of our writing club's newsletter, and a member of the board. My husband and I are part of a mentoring team through our church. I continue to write books, as well as do all my own marketing (as all small-time authors must do), blogging, and social media. First and foremost, I'm a wife, and a mom and step-mom to three teenage kids.

So how do I do it without completely falling apart? How do I manage to balance the have-tos of my life with the want-tos of my creative life? How do I keep from unraveling at the seams?

Let me pause here while I totally laugh out loud.

I have had my fair share of meltdowns. The biggest frustration, as many aspiring authors will tell you, is having to work a full-time job that has traveled so far from my passion just to make ends meet, when all I want to do is write books. Period. However, the bills have to be paid, and finding success through writing books takes time, patience, and a pinch of luck.

Until then, the full-time job stays. And moment by moment, I have to gather my sanity, remember what my ultimate goal is, and never give up.

That means, writing every day, even when I don't feel like it. It means finding inspiration in even the smallest of ways. It means staying organized and protecting my creative time. It means managing even the most mundane parts of my day-to-day life, and still striving to feed my creative soul.

The same goes for you. Your life may have taken a turn you didn't want. You may be spending more time doing the mundane, and have to fight to keep the creativity in your life. Keep fighting. Your art is worth it, and the world needs it.

My mission is to help you reach your goal.

So here we go. Are you ready to change the path you're on right now and step toward the creative life you've always wanted? Let's go on a journey.

Intro: Part 2

How to Use This Book

Before we start, here is what you can expect to learn, and how to best utilize this book to reclaim your creative soul.

I've separated this book into five sections, each one addressing different areas of your life that may need improving to make room for your craft. The first read-through is best done cover to cover. Once you've done that, I encourage you to re-read the sections that spoke to any issues you are currently facing, and apply the steps laid out to help you tackle these issues.

Here is a summary of each section in this book:

Section 1: Calming Techniques

The rest of the world is competing for your attention. If you're not careful, it can overwhelm the focus you need for your art. This section teaches you ways to detach from the busy-ness around you with ways to stay calm and tune in to the creative side of your soul.

Section 2: Soul Exercises

When things get too overwhelming, it probably means you haven't taken time for yourself. This section offers ways to reconnect with your soul and come back to center.

Section 3: Organization

Often when we are overwhelmed, it's because we have too many things coming at us without any sense of order. From managing your finances to organizing your personal space, and more, this section addresses ways you can create order to the everyday parts of your life so that you can find room for your craft.

Section 4: Boundaries

If you don't know how to protect your time and space, every other part of your life is going to try to manage it for you. This section teaches you how to say "no" when necessary, protect yourself against distractions, and lock in the time you need for your craft.

Section 5: Reclaim Your Creative Soul

Once you've created order around the rest of your life, it's time to make the most of your creativity. This section offers ways to be proactive with your craft and set goals to take you further with your artistic abilities.

At the end of every chapter, I have listed challenges to help you learn how to apply these tips to your life, separating them into three different levels of complexity. Some challenges are easy. Some require more thought and time.

You do not need to do every single challenge.

Decide for yourself how much time you want to spend on a specific issue, and go from there. You may even decide to hold off on challenges so that you can move through the book quickly in your first read-through. The choice is up to you, and this journey is yours.

And with that, let's begin.

Section 1

Calming Techniques

The first step to organizing your full-time life is to learn how to keep calm when the rest of the world is competing for your attention. The next three chapters share ways to tune out the noise from an overly busy world, find time to do the things that you love to do, and learn how to meditate on words of wisdom to keep yourself centered.

Chapter 1

Tuning Out the Noise

As a writer, one of my very favorite places to hang out is at a coffee shop. But not just any coffee shop. I love hanging out at Starbucks. I'm actually here right now, writing this chapter from a table within the store.

This place caters completely to people with laptops. There are plenty of tables near a plug (the all-valuable life source!) so I can write for hours on end. There are plenty of delicious foods and a never-ending supply of caffeine (another all-valuable life source!). The people are generally friendly, and the baristas never give me the evil eye if I take up a table long after I've finished drinking my coffee.

But one thing about Starbucks—it's really loud.

As I write this, there is a child throwing a temper tantrum while his parents decide what to buy for him to eat. The music is a touch too loud. There are people sitting behind me who seem to be sharing their conversation with the entire shop. The coffee machine is rattling. People are chatting away in line. And me? I'm wearing huge earphones with my music on blast in my ears to try to drown out the noise in the shop.

It's noisy here at Starbucks. But I'm here to avoid seeing my kids who will inevitably need something, my dog who will distract me as he hunts houseflies, my husband who might remind me of one or five chores I've been putting off, and to escape the need to do anything around the house that has nothing to do with writing. It might be noisy here, but it's louder at my house.

We live in a world filled with chatter. The alarm blares, and you get up. Maybe you keep the radio on while you get dressed, or you turn on the TV to watch the news. The coffee grinder whirs, and then the coffee pot starts dripping. Someone needs to be fed—a kid, maybe a cat. You make your lunch, and then get in the car to go to work, listening to music the whole time. The sound of chatter fills your office, as does the sound of clacking keys, ringing phones, and endless meetings. In my office, we have all that, plus the sound of police scanners announcing a string of emergencies over the airwaves. Leave the office, and there's traffic on the streets, airplanes in the sky, people yelling on the corner…. Go home and there's more noise as you are pulled in every direction to get dinner done, help the kids with homework, watch the news, check your email, peruse social media, and then, finally, go to bed so you can start again the next day.

But it goes much deeper than that. Not only are you surrounded by noise, it exists inside you, as well.

Unfortunately, this noise is much, much louder. It's the voice of your mother telling you all the things you've failed to do so far, or casting doubt on the things you want to try. It's the green-eyed monster who sees the success a friend of yours is having with seemingly no effort at all, while you are toiling away with little to no results. It's the note from the teacher who wants to talk about your child's strange habit of eating the tips off all the yellow crayons. It's the extra weight you see on the scale, and the nagging voice that reminds you about every carb you ate the day before. It's the guilt you feel about wanting to spend more time creating, when you *should* be doing something *much more productive with your time*—you know, like cutting the crusts off your kid's sandwich.

It's the list of should-dos running through your head. *I should do the laundry. I should organize my closet. I should call my friend. I should volunteer in my child's class. I should really exercise. I should walk the dog. I should do more for the environment. I should learn to eat better. I should mop the floor. I should learn to play the guitar. I should learn a new language. I should teach my kids a new language. I should....be doing anything except what I'm doing at this exact moment....*

And that's what it's really about. The way of the world has become go, go, GO. If you're not multi-tasking, you're doing it wrong, says the world. One of the most popular characteristics in an employee is how well they do more than one thing at the same time. And if you're a parent of

19

a toddler? Just try to do one thing at a time while those precious little monsters are under your care.

But the worst culprit? Your smartphone.

Wait! Don't shut this book. I, just like you, love my smartphone. Love isn't even a strong enough word. Without my smartphone, I'd be lost. It holds all my music, my photos, my checkbook, my to-do list, my social connection to friends, my email, a map so I don't get lost, a friend named Siri who caters to my every whim, a calculator so I can figure out what to leave for a tip, and my family's entire calendar. It wakes me up with a gentle song every morning. It has a weather app so I can decide what to wear each day. It allows me to read books when my Kindle isn't charged. It measures my running time so I can tell how much I'm improving (or rather, how slow I still am). It holds yoga videos so I can get all Zen-like at a moment's notice. And it has plenty of other features to ensure I won't ever get bored.

But that's the thing. I *still* get bored. I'll scroll through social media to see what everyone else is doing. I'll check my email, and then refresh the page to see if anything came through in the last thirty seconds. And repeat. I'll play pointless games. I'll check my bank account. I'll check my social media again. And, I'll be bored.

I know I'm not alone. Stand in line at the grocery store, and what are people doing? How about on the bus? What about in any situation that forces people to pause for a moment? They're staring at their phone, killing time by being somewhere else until they can actually *be* somewhere else.

Wild idea. What if we, you know, just enjoyed the moment we're in?

The smartphone has killed our ability to do nothing for a little while. Worse, it has limited our vision of the world around us. We're so busy looking into this tiny screen that we fail to see the beauty that surrounds us. We miss the little moments because we are paying attention to some noble cause our friend has posted on their Facebook wall, the cute video of puppies falling down stairs on YouTube, the amazing string of selfies your friend posted on Instagram, and the emails detailing the amount of money we can save if we just shop now.

Meanwhile, we are missing the moment a gust of wind picked up a leaf, turned it around in a mini tornado, and rested it gently back on the ground. We're missing the baby that's sitting three tables away, sneaking peeks at us while his mother spoon feeds him something orange from a jar. We are missing the smile from a perfect stranger who catches our eye before looking away. We're missing the way the clouds are perfectly scattered across the sky, almost as if they are holding up the blue with all their might. We are missing the moment, a moment we will never get back again, because we're too busy "multi-tasking."

But tell me, are we *really* multi-tasking? I mean, are we really in tune with what's going on around us when we are plugged in?

This, my friends, along with every single other noise in your life, is the very first thing that is keeping you away from your creativity.

To reclaim your creativity, you will need to find a way to escape the noise in your life. Admittedly, I know that this is easier said than done. As the parent of three teenagers and a teenage dog, noise surrounds me. At all waking hours of the day, our home is filled with the sounds of video games, TV, barking, rap star impressions (don't ask), chicken impressions (seriously, don't ask), and regular intervals of "What's for dinner?" and "I just need you to sign this for school tomorrow." And being that I am still sitting inside a noisy Starbucks with my music blasting in my ears, I still haven't escaped the noise.

But finding pockets of quiet time is vital to both your art and your health. And it's not impossible. When you're driving, turn the radio off and just drive. If you take the bus, just sit still and be. While you are washing the dishes, focus on the task and nothing else. Take a walk around your neighborhood on your own, unaccompanied by music. Close yourself in the bathroom and take ten minutes to yourself. Sit in a park and just watch the scenery. Lie in the grass and look up at the sky. Refrain from picking up your phone whenever you have nothing to do, when you want to avoid a certain feeling, or when you just want to be entertained. Dedicate yourself to being in the moment.

Most important—BREATHE. Just breathe. Don't think. Don't do. Just take one breath in, let it out, and repeat.

CHALLENGE YOURSELF

Baby Step: Every day, take ten minutes to yourself to breathe and do nothing. This only counts if you are uninterrupted, so find a place and time when you're sure you can be totally alone. During this time, thoughts you did not invite in will inevitably show up for a visit—you know, all those "should dos" and the nagging reminders of everything you're *not* doing. Let them know that you'll be available for their abuse in ten minutes, and then just focus on your breathing. One breath in. One breath out. Repeat.

Strive for three times a day, but even once a day is better than nothing.

Level Up: Along with the above step, turn the Internet off your smartphone for one day. Prohibit yourself from using your phone at all as a source of entertainment on this day, and only use it as a phone. Make a mental note of every time you reach for it to avoid boredom or to entertain yourself, and refrain from caving in. Remember, it's only for one day. You've got this!

Be Hardcore: Along with finding quiet time, enjoy a total tech-free day! This is harder than you think. This means leaving your phone at home (I know! But you'll survive! I promise!), staying away from the computer, avoiding television, turning off the radio, etc. While away from all your technology, pay attention to how you feel. Does your head feel clearer? Are you noticing things you missed before? I encourage you to document this experience through journaling, or some other creative way of expressing your feelings.

Chapter 2

Do What You Love

I remember the day I told my editor I didn't think I could continue writing my newspaper column anymore. I told her I needed a break from the article, as the more technical side of my job had become too crazy for me to keep up with the creative parts. We decided on a three-month hiatus, and agreed to revisit the issue at the end of that time.

As you may remember from earlier in this book, having my own newspaper column was my dream. So why was I throwing in the towel? Easy—I was overwhelmed. There were so many components to my job, I had nothing left in me to write something witty every single week. I felt like taking this one huge thing off my plate would help to lighten my load, both workwise and emotionally.

But it only made things worse.

Years later, I look back at that time, and just want to shake myself by the shoulders. Before giving that column up, I was saying "yes" every time someone came to me with a task that need completing, even if I didn't really want to do it. If someone needed their load lightened, I was right there to take it on for them. If a new project was introduced, I didn't hesitate when asked to complete it. If a customer needed assistance, I took the call, even if I was swamped with work. I had many hats that didn't fit my job description, and sometimes I wasn't sure what my job description really was.

But I felt like this was what I was supposed to do to be a good worker. I wanted to be the person my boss could come to about anything, and the person my coworkers felt they could depend on. I thought that maybe if I said "yes" with a smile to everything that was handed to me, I would eventually be trusted enough to do what I really wanted to—write exclusively for the newspaper.

Two problems existed in this way of thinking. First, I never made it clear that this was what I wanted to do, or even helped to come up with a game plan on how I could eventually move into a writing role at the newspaper. Second, I was saying "yes" to so many things for other people, I was eventually forced to say "no" to many of the things I wanted to do.

Soon, the things I didn't want to do became my whole entire job.

It's kind of sneaky how this happened. I made it my mission to get all the mundane, boring parts of my job done first so that I could save the best parts of my job for last. I'm sure you see where this is going. As the boring tasks became bigger and more involved, I had to keep pushing the fun parts further and further down the list. Eventually, they even started to fall off my list completely. First was the parenting website I ran. Then the parenting columns. Eventually I gave up going to features meeting, missing the chance to take on any new articles at all. In a sense, I voluntarily gave up all the parts that made me look forward to going to work, and traded them in for all the parts that made me have to give myself a pep talk before I even walked in the door.

Three months after my hiatus from the parenting column, I let my editor know I was ready to begin again. But the damage was done. A month later and the newspaper stripped my column from its pages to make room for other things. Part of this was due to a redesign. But I'm pretty sure my brief hiatus made it easy to imagine the newspaper without my column there ever again.

As creatives, it's so easy for us to not take our craft seriously enough to put it first—to see that time as voluntary, and give it up easily when "more important things" show their face. That time is the first thing we give up when a friend needs our assistance, the chores are piling up, or the boss wants you to work extra hours.

But your creative time should NOT be treated as expendable! I'm not saying those other needs aren't important. But if you give up the things you love doing the most, you are giving up the parts of your life that feed your soul. If you give the majority of your time to the tasks you dread the most, you run the risk of those things taking over every facet of your life.

Trust me, you don't want this.

A few months ago, I was feeling overwhelmed at the path my life had taken. My job felt especially soul-sucking, and all of the creativity in my life was seriously lacking. I couldn't even think of how to get out of my rut, and felt completely wound up, frazzled…spun. The only thing I could think of doing was to enlist the help of my family.

I took two large pieces of cardboard and stuck them to my wall. On one piece I wrote, "What is stressing you out?" On the other I wrote, "What makes you feel calm?" Then I put a note on both of them, instructing the members of my family to add thoughts under each question.

Throughout the week, the cardboard turned into a jumbled mess of words. The only rule was to be honest, but refrain from being mean. Other than that, the sky was the limit for what each family member could add to the list.

Here are a few things that stress the members of my family out:

- Long lines
- Deadlines
- Traffic
- Bossy people
- Arguments
- Being late

- Disrespect
- Feeling judged
- Clutter
- Calories
- Writer's block
- Money/debt
- Too many emails
- Dishonesty
- Public speaking

And here is what brings my family peace:

- Cuddling with the dog
- Deep breaths
- Creative writing
- Journaling
- Riding bikes
- The ocean
- Coloring
- Hiking
- Showing affection
- Hanging out with friends
- Exercising
- Drawing
- Taking photos
- Listening to music

I took a picture of each of these lists and saved them to my phone. And I refer to them often. The stress list serves as a reminder that I'm not alone. Occasionally I'll even add to these lists, putting a name to the very thing that is causing me to feel pulled in all directions. The calm list gives me ideas on how to come back to center, reminding me to take the time for the things I love doing.

Somewhere in the time between being a child and being adult, we learned that life was about giving priority to the stuff we hate. As kids, we're told to eat our vegetables before we can have dessert. We're told to finish our chores before we can play outside. We're told to do our homework before we can turn on the TV. We're made to give up recess until we've learned to sit still in class. We're told that work is supposed to be boring and dreadful, because that's just life.

I say NO!

Okay, I also say that most of those things really are important. We *should* eat our vegetables (but only the ones we like!). We *should* finish our chores (but it shouldn't take all day!). We *should* do our homework (but take mini breaks in between!). However, recess is allowed, jobs can be fun, and being an adult doesn't have to suck.

Here's the thing. If you don't make time for the things you love, you're going to end up miserable, burnt out, depleted, depressed, unfulfilled, uninspired…. Should I go on? We all have stuff that *needs* to get done. But if your daily routine is starting to look more like all work and no play, you're going to end up in a rut that isn't easy to get out of. If you don't make time for the things that feed your soul, life will start to feel meaningless. Your art, the very thing that once defined you, will start to feel like a burden to you. It will become something you resent as inspiration becomes harder to find.

However, doing the things you love will lighten that load considerable. Suddenly, you'll see the light in life, and have something to look forward to each day. Not only that, but doing the things you love can give you the energy to tackle the more mundane parts of your life.

Let's take a walk through the memories of your past, shall we? Go back to your childhood days, the time when play ruled your life and the fun was endless. What was something that you would stop in your tracks for? What did you absolutely love doing? Were you a coloring book fanatic? Were you into building structures out of Legos? Perhaps you loved roller skating around the block, or playing jump rope with friends. Right now, I want you to think about your favorite activity, the one that made your whole insides feel like they were bigger than your outsides. Got it? Good. Hold on to that for a moment, it's going to come in handy in just a few paragraphs.

For me, it was creating "Indian Villages" out of algae and sticks in the creek that ran by our family's home. My sisters and I would spend hours in the grass, collecting the slimy green sludge, and breaking sticks into tiny pieces for the houses. We'd build teepees and coat them with the algae until the creek was lined by a whole entire mini village. We'd weave stories out of our village, adding characters to the little town we had created. Our imaginations were running full steam ahead as we built an entire land out of moss, sticks, and dreams on the banks of our neighborhood creek.

Back in those days, we took the time for the things we loved. Granted, we had a lot less required of us back then. But we still managed to fit in fun with our homework and making our bed and washing up for dinner.

Just because we're adults doesn't mean we need to stop having fun. In fact, having fun should be a requirement for being adult. After all, haven't we earned the fun parts of life?

CHALLENGE YOURSELF

Baby Step: Remember those two lists I told you about? I want you to make your own. On one list, write down everything that is stressing you out and pulling you in all directions. Leave nothing out. This list is just for you, so be as honest as you can. When you are done with that, write another list of the things that make you happy or keep you calm. List things like your favorite activities, your favorite color, the books you love to read, the music that makes you want to dance, etc. Keep writing until you run out of things to write. And then, keep that list handy so that you can add to it when more things come to you.

Level Up: After you've written both of your lists, choose something from your calm list to focus on every day. Sometimes it might be listening to a song. Other times it's visiting the beach. The level of difficulty depends on your needs. The only requirement is that it needs to be something that makes you feel happy.

Be Hardcore: Here's where that childhood memory comes into play. I want you to do the first two steps. But I also want you to revisit your childhood by doing that one favorite thing you loved to do growing up. Grab a coloring book and start coloring. Build you own "Indian Village." Roller skate around your neighborhood. Create a tower out of Legos. You're going to feel silly, and you might have people look at you strange. Ignore everyone. In this moment, you are a kid once again, and your only job is to have fun.

Chapter 3

The Power of Words

Almost a decade ago, a friend of mine handed me the book, *Eat. Pray. Love.,* by Elizabeth Gilbert, and told me to read it. I set that book down on my nightstand and promptly forgot about it. I know I saw it there every night before I went to bed, but it was starting to blend in with the furniture.

Eventually, I did pick it up. I don't remember what prompted me to do so. But I do know that once I started reading, I couldn't put it down. The book spoke to me where I was—a woman struggling to know my place in the world as a single mother when the world only seemed to cater to couples. At the time that I read this book, I was still trying to figure out my identity. I had been divorced for two years at that point, and I was stuck in between wanting to celebrate my freedom, and wanting to find someone who loved me. I had been searching all the wrong places to find my personal meaning, trying to lean on everything and everyone outside of me to give myself a purpose.

We all know how well that works.

In *Eat. Pray. Love.*, Liz starts her journey on the bathroom floor of the home she had just bought with her husband. She had reached the terrifying place where she knew her marriage wasn't working. She kept finding herself there night after night after night, mourning the path her life had taken and trying to figure things out on her own. But on this night, things were different. This time she began to pray.

The story goes on after her marriage has ended. She's taken a lover, and has immersed her whole being into this other person. All of her love, her fears, her hurt, her anger, her meaning, her purpose, her failed marriage…it all becomes tangled into the soul of this other tortured artist. Together, they share this dramatic love affair that has more to do with avoiding the pain of what's real than what the other person is actually capable of offering. As the unhealthiness of this relationship becomes clear, Liz decides it's time to retreat. The relationship is put on hold while she begins a year-long adventure around the world.

And here is where the story picks up, the one that has sent many a divorcee on a soul-searching expedition to lands far away.

The adventure starts in Italy, which is only the most perfect place to go when you are filled with sorrow and angst. I mean, if the gorgeous scenery and exquisite art can't take away your pain, you can at least *eat* your feelings. There in Italy, Liz found peace within friendship, connecting with a motley crew of interesting characters who surround her with love and support. These friends offer her good times without the messiness of romance or having to answer for her past. Italy was where she was able to get over that hump of self-focused misery, and where she began to see the joy all around her.

From there, she traveled to India, leaving the land of over-indulgence for the land of no indulgence. It was here that she learned to stop seeking her worth in outer things, and started to build her worth within herself. It is also here where she found closure with the unhealthy romance, ending it with grace and love.

After months of meditation, silence, and self-discovery, Liz ends her journey in Indonesia. This is the place where she finds romantic love. Not only is she able to recognize it, but she's now capable of accepting it.

There's a reason why this book spent so much time on the New York Times Best Seller List. In Liz Gilbert's dedication to authenticity, she reached an extraordinarily large number of readers who were on a variety of life paths. Some were divorced. Some were looking for a life change. Some were leaving one decade to enter the next. Some were thinking about having children. Some were facing the fear of their children leaving the nest.

From an outer appearance, this story was about the journey from America to Italy, and then India, and finally Indonesia. But the true story was the transformation that took place inside of Liz. It was in *that* story where we all resonated. We found a friend who said, "Here's how I made a royal mess of my life, and here's how I got myself out of that mess. Here's the beauty that surfaced out of utter chaos. Now, let's find out where your beauty lies, okay?"

As a human, I find inspiration from a good story. But as a writer, I find power in the storyteller—particularly in the way words are laid out to stir up certain emotions, make a connection, and send you on a journey without ever leaving the comfort of your home. Because of this, I'm a huge reader. In fact, I'm one of those people who can read a book several times through, just because of the way it made me feel as I read it.

Traveling Mercies, by Anne Lamott, taught me that it's okay to be imperfect, and that even messy faith can be deep, fulfilling, and inspiring. *The Monk Downstairs,* by Tim Farrington, and *The Lovely Bones,* by Alice Sebold, painted such vivid imagery, that each word drew me deeper and deeper within the pages. The *Harry Potter* series created a world of magic that stayed with me even when I wasn't reading. *Peter Pan* echoed my life as I grew, encapsulating the ache of trying to pause in that place between childhood and adult.

Reading books is an inexpensive way to travel the world. Books have the ability to teach you new things, and to expand your imagination. They offer insights you might never have explored otherwise, and introduce you to all sorts of interesting characters that can sometimes feel like friends. Books have the power to reach you where you are, comfort you, offer you entertainment, and fill you with emotions.

Like *Eat. Pray. Love.* is for me, there is the perfect soul book somewhere out there for you. But the only way you can find it is to *start reading*.

I know. Reading takes time. Like many of you, I found it hard to fit reading into my adult life. As a kid, my nose was always in a book. But as an adult, my love of reading kind of fell to the wayside to make room for other things that went along with adulting. However, to be a writer, I realized I really needed to be a reader, as well. I couldn't expect to *write* books people resonated with if I wasn't *reading* books that resonated with me. So I began reading anything that interested me, grabbing hold of any book that was suggested as a good read, and diving straight in. But I didn't just kick back and enjoy the story. Instead, I paid attention to how the author was telling the story. How did she introduce the characters? How did he show that the character was feeling sad? What did I like about the way the author described the scenery? What would I like to change about it?

Being a writer has changed the way I read forever. And that's okay. What it's also done is re-ignite my passion for a good book. Now, I am always in the middle of a novel. Sometimes I'm in the middle of several books at one time. Sometimes I wish there was more time in the day so I could just continue reading whatever story I'm in the middle of.

I wouldn't have it any other way.

If you're not a reader, I encourage you to start. It doesn't even have to all be fiction, though I encourage you to read *some* fiction. Read books about your craft to gain a deeper understanding. Read books that stretch your imagination. Read books on the Best Seller List. Read books that you've never heard of before, but appear to be something you'd want to finish to the end. If a book doesn't resonate with you (and you should always give it a three-chapter chance), set it down and start a different one. After all, there's no sense wasting time on something you don't enjoy. Just read, and then read again.

Books aren't the only place to find words that resonate and inspire. Another powerful source of comforting words is from the lyrics of your favorite songs. A simple song has the ability to transport you to another place, evoke strong emotions, wrap you in its meanings, envelop you with its melody, and capture you like almost nothing else.

Of course, songs also affect people in different ways. For example, there's my intense love for the band, Radiohead. If Thom Yorke sings it, I'm listening to it. Some of his songs are so incredibly deep. His lyrics dance circles around my tiny little issues, celebrate moments of angst, and make me wish I were a bit more of a tortured soul. The intensity of his music grabs hold of me like nothing else. I could lay on my back with headphones on, listening to each Radiohead album one right after the other. And then, I could listen to them all over again.

When I first fell in love with my husband, I wanted to let him know just how much I loved him in a very special way. I needed to share with him something completely from the heart. *I needed to share my Radiohead.* But not just any Radiohead album would do. It had to be the one album that spoke to my soul like no other. I had to share Radiohead's "Kid A" album.

For those of you who are familiar with "Kid A," you are probably shaking your head and laughing. For those of you who aren't familiar, let me enlighten you. One does not simply dive into Radiohead through "Kid A." It's far too eclectic for that. "Kid A" is full of deep tracks, the ones where Thom Yorke went off on a tangent and never came back. The album is brilliant, full of musical genius, one that tells a different story every time I listen to it. But if you've never heard Radiohead before, it's the album that will make you swear off Radiohead forever.

At the time, I didn't realize this. I only thought I was giving my husband a piece of my heart, wrapped in the shape of a carefully burned CD. He thought I was giving him an album of cat screeches and impossible-to-understand mumblings. It totally ruined any chance of him liking Radiohead at all. And now we have to agree to disagree on the brilliance of my favorite band.

Side note: If you are now curious about Radiohead and aren't sure where to start, "Pablo Honey" is a safe jumping off point, and is the band's first mainstream album. But my personal safe favorite is the album, "In Rainbows."

Back to Radiohead. The reason I was drawn to this band was not only their amazing way with music, but the way the lyrics never plainly said what they were about. You have to read between the lines to understand the full meaning. And when you do, the meaning is so crystal clear, and so human.

Isn't that the way with almost any amazing artist?

To be truly honest, there's a lot of crap music out there in the world today. But there is a lot of really amazing music out there, too. There are true poets putting notes to their words, creating a symphony of emotion that's hard to match. Songwriters and musicians are true artists, and if you're one of them, my hat goes off to you. It's not easy to put together so many components to create something that draws people in and makes them want to stay awhile.

What are some of the songs you currently enjoy? Have you ever thought about *why* you enjoy them? Does it go deeper than the beat or the music? Have you stopped to listen to what the songwriter is actually saying?

The final source of powerful words I want to touch on is poetry. To me, poetry stands somewhere between storytelling and songwriting. It's a story told in pleasant form. It's a song without words. It's placing your subject under a microscope and zooming way in until that tiny object appears larger than life. Poetry is a meditation of sorts, a rhythmic dance with words that can offer peace, or can shake things up.

Before I started writing books, I wasn't quite sure where to begin. I kept starting and stopping, unsure what to write as soon as my fingers came near a keyboard. You know what loosened things up?

Poetry.

Let me make this perfectly clear—I am not a poet. I'm also not an avid reader of poetry. But I do have a few favorite poets, as well as a few favorite pieces of poetry. So I figured, what the hey, and I started writing.

The stuff I was producing wasn't epic. But it wasn't half bad, either. I started sharing my poetry in an online forum with other poets. Soon I was an active part of this little community of writers who shared poetry with each other who offered praise along with tips on making each poem stronger. My writing ability grew stronger, and so did my confidence in my ability.

My collection of poetry grew over the years. Through it, I got out all the angst I was feeling over being a single mother, the yearning for steamy romance, the anger over my lot in life, the questions I had about faith, the love I had for my children, the quiet moments when I felt God…. I revealed my soul in these poems, holding nothing back. They became my veiled diary entries, the words I wrote that said one thing in black and white, but held many notes of grey only the most diligent reader could uncover.

What started out as an exercise for writing ended up being something I was quite proud of. Not only that, but by loosening my prose with poetry, I was able to go on to produce novels. But I didn't stop there. I realized that these personal poems deserved to be bound in a book, as well. I collected all of my favorite poems and published a book of poetry called, *Everything I Am Not Saying*. I don't heavily promote this book at all, and it's only sold a handful of copies. But that's okay with me. The real purpose behind that book was to be able to hold my poetry in my hands and see where I was, and how far I've come since those poems were written.

Not everyone is into poetry. Most poets are not getting rich off their words. Poetry books are not flying off the shelves. However, poets are part of this secret society of artists— a community amongst themselves that hold the mysteries of language not understood by many. They're kind of like the Radiohead of the writing world. Poetry holds so much power within just a few lines.

I end this chapter now with a few poems written by poets I love and admire, as well as one of my own.

Respect
By Jean Wong (author of *Sleeping With the Gods*)

Respect sits quietly in the corner
like a school boy with a dunce cap.
Whenever she is summoned,
children roll their eyes and yawn.
She fights to gain footing,
enlisting flags and churches,

finds only mockery and pretense
like confetti at her feet.
She must wait patiently
for the decrepit and aged.
Then they sit with her
on a park bench,
shake their head,
and tsk.

Waiting
By Michelle Wing (author of *Body on the Wall*)

Your words come through the phone,
and I sweep them up with gentle hands
to drop them one by one into a glass jar,
preserving them
like peaches.
Anticipating succulence,
I wade slowly through spring days
into August heat,
heavy with longing. At last
I set the jar on the porch to warm
in three o'clock sunlight,
then serve you plump promises
in cool blue and white bowls.

Vulnerable

By Crissi Langwell (From *Everything I Am Not Saying*)

The sky is a rosy pink
   lit ablaze by strange fires
      flush with a romantic glow.
I sit here with my pen
looking out at the hazy sky
wrapped up in a bathrobe
      having washed your scent from my skin
and feverish from the heat
not to mention the shock
      from the longing that won't rub clean.

I didn't see it coming
and I am suddenly silent
unsure of the words
that will wrap around
      whatever it is they need to cover.

The sky is on fire and surely it is my fault.

The tangling of my breath and my soul
      that was carried out on the sleeve of your jacket
left me vulnerable in a way
      I'm not quite comfortable with.

But I watched as you walked away

keeping silent as you turned the corner
overcome with regret
either for not speaking up
or for being so careless in the first place.

And now all I can do
is watch the sky turn from pink to purple
and then fade to black
as our scene ends in your mind
and hits replay in mine.

CHALLENGE YOURSELF

Baby Step: Pick one of your favorite songs. Gather the lyrics and go through each line one by one. What is the songwriter trying to say? Does it change your view of the song?

Level Up: Write poetry for an hour. For inspiration, read a few poems by some of the greats. My personal favorites are "Somewhere I Have Never Travelled," by e.e. cummings, "I'm Nobody," by Emily Dickinson, and anything by Billy Collins. Another great place to look is at WritersCafe.org, a place where many poets share amazing works. Then start writing. Your poetry does not have to rhyme, and it doesn't have to be a certain length. It can be anything you want it to be.

Go Hardcore: Turn off the TV this week and use that time for reading a good novel. When you're finished with that book, pick up another and read some more. Strive to read at least one new novel a month.

Section 2

Soul Exercises

So much in this world is competing for your attention and drive. You're encouraged to try harder, work faster, and be better. You're being marketed to at all hours of the day. You keep trying to reach that place where you don't have to work so hard, but it always seem just out of your grasp. And the things you are passionate about get lost in the shuffle.

This section shares ways to get back in touch with your soul and everything that refreshes it by preparing your mind, offering ways to nurture yourself, and teaching you how to take a personal soul retreat.

Chapter 4

Preparing Your Mind

Do you remember in Chapter 1 when I talked about the importance of tuning out the noise and finding quiet? In this first chapter on soul exercises, we're going to take it one step further. We will now focus on stilling the mind through three techniques I've personally found peace through: meditation, contemplative reading, and journaling.

Meditation

Clearing your mind and dropping into a meditative state is not so easy for everyone. At least, that's how it's been in my experience. I find that silence can sometimes be the loudest sound, and my inner voice loves to chatter when I'm trying to be still. However, I've also learned to be gentle with myself about it. Meditation takes practice to clear the mind successfully. Even the most dedicated Yogis can still experience moments of disconnect from their focus.

The argument for meditation is pretty solid. We live in a busy world, where everything is fast-paced and the news of today is old by noon. Technology has kept us connected to each other at all times. Traffic jams are inevitable. Work is non-stop. Everything is go, go, go; move, move, move; now, now, now. But with meditation, time slows down and the world is put on pause while you come back to center.

When you meditate, you are giving yourself permission to set aside everything that is demanding your attention, whether warranted or not. You are telling each distracting thought that you will come back for it later, but right now, you get to have a moment for yourself. By meditating, you are taking a break from your busy-ness, granting yourself a mini-vacation so that you can come back to the real world refreshed and ready to start anew.

Even science approves of meditation. Multiple studies have shown that meditation can improve your thinking, help you process and control your emotions, change your perception of pain, focus in a high-stress environment, increase your body awareness, reduce the effects of sickness, and boost your ability to pay attention and focus.

The simple explanation on how to meditate is to clear your mind and breathe for a length of time. But that's not self-explanatory. I mean, how exactly does one clear their mind, especially when the inner chatter just won't stop?

Like I said, it's not easy. But it's not impossible, either. Here are the steps you should take to lead yourself to a meditative state.

First, create a sitting practice. Choose a time and a space where you won't be interrupted, and then establish a specific amount of time you plan to meditate. Check your posture and make sure your spine is straight. You can lean against a wall if that makes it easier for you. Then, with a straight spine, relax every other part of your body. Let yourself become soft. Focus on each body part one by one: start with your scalp, then to your face, loosen your jaw, relax your neck, unclench your shoulders and hands, untighten your belly, soften your leg muscles and your toes. Breathe into each part of your body as you focus on letting go.

Once you are relaxed, focus on one thing, and one thing only. Start with your breath. Focus on taking one breath in, and then letting it out. Breathe in. Then breathe out. Do this for at least ten breaths. You can continue focusing on your breath, or you can move to something else. Other things to focus on can be your body's reaction to each breath, as in the rise of your chest or the expansion of your belly, or you can focus on your body's sensation as you relax even more into your meditation. Your mind will want to wander. Don't get frustrated. Just make note of this distraction, and then gently lead your mind back to your focus. Keep going until your time is up.

You may experience several interruptions while you are trying to keep your focus. This can include random thoughts, or even just letting your thoughts control what you are focusing on. You might also find yourself wishing you were in a more peaceful state than you are in the moment, or more relaxed than you're able to get. Other interruptions include aversion to the process, negative feelings, restlessness, sleepiness, or doubt that you'll ever achieve a meditative state. Simply guide your mind back to your focus each time you find yourself drifting. However, if the interruption or emotion you are experiencing is too strong, submit to the feeling completely. While you can't predict how this interruption will play out, do know that it will dissipate eventually. Once it's gone, return to your meditation until your time is up.

Maintain a regular practice for meditation by sitting every single day, preferably at a consistent time. The best times to meditate are when you wake up, whenever you feel stressed, during your lunch break, or after work. The one time you *shouldn't* meditate, however, is right before bed. It's too easy to mix sleep with meditation, and your mind should be completely alert. Short meditation sessions are completely acceptable, and it's beneficial if you can meditate several times a day. You can practice by yourself, in a meditation group, or with a friend or family member.

You can find resources on meditation at the back of this book.

Contemplative Reading

In the Christian faith, Lectio Divina is the Latin phrase for Divine Reading. This form of contemplative reading is the spiritual practice of meditating on God's word, established in the 6th century by Saint Benedict, and eventually formalized by the Carthusian monk, Guigo II. The process has four parts: read a passage of scripture, meditate on it, pray about it, and then contemplate what it's truly saying. The idea isn't to treat the scripture as text in a book to be studied and dissected, but to treat the scripture as the Living Word, letting the words speak their meaning to the reader.

As a Christian, this practice is one that draws me closer to God. It's a beautiful way to be still for a moment and hear what wisdom God has for me, or even the message he is sending me through one word or idea.

In this exercise, I am borrowing from this Christian practice, but I'm giving it a more secular spin. While Lectio Divina is about scriptural reading, I believe all wisdom can be absorbed through contemplation. However, you have to be so careful about the wisdom upon which you choose to meditate. As we all know, even well-intentioned advice isn't always the best advice. Before you choose wisdom to contemplate, read it over several times to be sure this is something that sits right with your heart. If it does, here are the steps you should take with these words.

Read the passage several times through. As you read, pay attention to any words or phrases that stand out to you more in the text. Repeat those phrases several times, both in your head and whispered on your lips. Close your eyes. Breathe the passage in. Breathe the passage out. Meditate on this and allow your body to absorb the passage. Do this until you feel the moment is right. With your eyes closed, mentally thank the person who wrote this passage, and thank the Universe for sending this passage your way. Spend as much time as you need in this gratitude. When you are done, write down the message this passage gave you, and anything else about the experience that moved you.

There are many different places you can find words of wisdom. It can be passages from an inspirational book. It can be a quote. It can be religious text. It can be a moving line in a song or poem. The possibilities are endless. The only rule is that it needs to be something that initially speaks to you when you come across it. That is when you know it has a deeper message for you to uncover through contemplative reading.

To get you started, here are a few quotes you may want to choose to contemplate. You can find more text at crissilangwell.com/free-resources-for-creative-souls.

"We are shaped by our thoughts; we become what we think. When the mind is pure, joy follows like a shadow that never leaves." – Buddha

"Be strong and courageous! Do not be afraid or discouraged. For the Lord your God is with you wherever you go." Bible, Joshua 1:9

"The quieter you become, the more you can hear." – Ram Dass

"Being deeply loved by someone gives you strength, while loving someone deeply gives you courage." – Lao Tzu

"If I can stop one heart from breaking, I shall not live in vain; If I can ease one life the aching, or cool one pain, or help one fainting robin unto his nest again, I shall not live in vain." – Emily Dickinson, poem "If I Can Stop One Heart from Breaking."

Journaling

I am ending this chapter on one of my very favorite ways to get in touch with my soul—journaling. It's probably not a surprise that a writer would enjoy journaling so much. But it wasn't always this way.

My life has always included some form of writing. I write books, I write articles, and I often write blog posts. But journaling? What was the point? No one was going to see what I wrote, so it felt kind of like a wasted effort.

I almost missed out on one of the greatest soul training exercises.

The thing about journaling is that *it's only for you.* You can be truly authentic in what you're writing, speaking truth you probably wouldn't want to share on a public forum.

This allows you to process feelings you may be bottling up, address frustrations that might go unmentioned, and solve problems that are plaguing you. There's no need to censor yourself in a journal because there is no one to offend.

I find that when I journal, I'm able to put things in perspective. Having my thoughts laid out in front of me allows me the ability to see things clearer than when I'm just letting my thoughts spin inside my head. Before I start writing, these thoughts are like a swarm of angry bees, stinging me with fragments of ideas without anything tangible to grasp. But when I pick up a pen and start writing, it's like the swarm simmers down, traveling through my pen to the paper one by one. Many past dilemmas I couldn't solve have been worked out by simply writing about them. It offers clarity to an unclear situation, and peace to chaos. Journaling has become a form of therapy for me.

Most of all, I am documenting my growth in every area of my life when I journal. It's amazing to look back through my journals to see how far I've come. Likewise, it offers me a clear answer that things need to change when I'm still writing about certain issues months later without any resolve. My journal has become the check and balance to my life, holding me accountable to the journey I'm on and the path where I'm headed.

There are times when I journal that a censored version of my entry will end up in my blog (or even in this book!). But, for the most part, my journal is the place where only

I am allowed, when I can be my most true self, and when I can clear my head of mental clutter.

Your journal can also be just for you. However, I get that it can feel like an adolescent Dear Diary session, or even just a laundry list of what you did that day, if you're not accustomed to writing down your feelings. If you're having a hard time knowing what to write in a journal, consider treating it more like a letter to a friend. One of my favorite examples of using a journal as letters to someone else was in the book, *The Good Luck of Right Now*, by Matthew Quick. In this fictional story, Quick details the life of Bartholomew, a man who was born mentally handicapped and lives with his single mother. When his mother dies, Bartholomew has to figure out how to navigate the world on his own. A "Free Tibet" letter he discovered from Richard Gere, coupled with the fact that his mother called him Richard in her final days, seemed somewhat of a cosmic sign to Bartholomew. He began keeping a journal, using it to write letters to his new "friend," Richard Gere (side note: I often wonder if Richard Gere has read this book, and what he thinks about being such an integral part of the storyline without ever showing his face within the pages once). The entire book consists of Bartholomew's letters to Gere, and his transformation from beginning to end is incredible.

If writing a journal entry doesn't seem to work for you, consider writing letters to someone else. You can even pick your favorite celebrity, a family member, or even write letters to God. There are no rules in journaling, and it's a practice you may grow to love.

CHALLENGE YOURSELF

Baby Step: Keep a journal every day this week. It doesn't have to be anything fancy. It can be as simple as a spiral notebook, or it can be as elaborate as a leather bound journal. At the end of your day, document what happened, and how you felt during the day. Or write in your journal at the start of the day, documenting what you are struggling with and what your intentions are for the next 24 hours. If you find it hard to know what to write, consider writing it to someone, like your favorite actor or artist, a family member, or even a spiritual being.

Level Up: Along with journaling, practice contemplative reading. You can even incorporate this into your journaling session. Choose a passage that speaks to you, then read it through several times and focus on the parts that begin to stand out to you. Meditate on those parts of the passage. Then mentally thank the creator of these words and journal the message you received from the text.

Be Hardcore: Practice meditation for twenty minutes every day this week. Strive for more than once a day, but meditate at least once a day.

Chapter 5

Treat Yourself

Our worst enemy can often be ourselves. We're the first person to find fault in our appearance, doubt our abilities, and assume everyone is better than us. When I look back at some of the things I've said about myself—*you're fat, other authors are so much better at this than you, no one wants to hear what you have to say, you're not as smart as your coworkers, your book sucks, you could never pull off that look, no one likes you*…. I would never say anything like that to other people. So, why do I think it's okay to say those things to myself?

We, as artists, are probably the hardest on ourselves. It's so easy to bash what we've created, even when other people recognize the magnificence of our creation. But with art comes a sort of madness, and many of us are on the verge of throwing in the towel, certain that someone is going to discover that we're just a hack who's pretending to get by. Anytime we think we have something figured out, our inner critic (let's call it "Marge," and give her a smoker's voice, just for kicks) comes breezing in, pointing out every flaw and imperfection. If we dare to make our art public, it gets worse. We build our worth on the feedback from others, and believe we are only as good as the reviews we receive. As soon as a bad review comes in, even one that's only slightly negative, "Marge" repeats that criticism so we're sure to take notice. Soon, all we hear is that bad review. It's almost like every other good thing that was said about our art was never said at all.

There's something I need to tell you. **You are a brilliant human being with a soul too big to be contained.** This is why you are an artist. Your art is your way of sharing your expanding soul with the world. If art brings you fulfillment, it's because you were meant to be an artist. People find joy in your creations, and this world would be bland without them.

But even saying that, I recognize that the only way you will ever be able to let go of "Marge" (or to at least learn to contain that saucy wench) is if you learn to fall in love with yourself.

You guys, things are about to get mushy in here. You've been warned.

The first step is to stop slamming yourself. Right this very moment, I want you to promise me that you'll make a valiant effort to stop negativity in its tracks, especially if it's not helpful. The moment that "Marge" pipes in with unsolicited feedback, I want you to kindly tell her that you don't need her help right now, and you're doing just fine on your own. You need to be stronger than feisty old "Marge," and let her know who the boss is.

Of course, dominating your inner critic is near impossible, unless you have the right tools in your belt. In this case, the right tools would be solid proof that you are perfectly capable as an artist—the things you are good at doing, the characteristics you possess that draw people in, the training or life experiences you've had that contribute to your expertise, the products of your creativity.... This list is as long as the talents, experiences, products and values you can claim as your own.

So, what are those things for you? The only way you can know is if you list out each of these items, adding them to a list of brag-worthy things about you. Don't be shy, it's not like you need to show this list to anyone. In this moment, give yourself permission to be proud of yourself. Are you nice? Are you funny? Put those on there. How about if you're organized? Or maybe you're like me and rock an ironclad budget. Add those skills to your list. If you run out of things, consider asking other people like your spouse or your best friend. There's no shame in it. After all, you'd do the same for them, wouldn't you?

Once you've finalized your list, study it. Memorize it. Own it. This is YOUR list. You are good at these things. This list contains the very reasons why you are wonderful, talented, unique, and completely capable. And when "Marge" comes back from her smoke break to give you an earful, kindly hold up your list and remind her that you've got this. Then tell her to go home.

So now that you love yourself, it's time to take yourself out on date (I warned you about the mushiness). Yes. I am seriously telling you to date yourself. This might feel a little uncomfortable, but bear with me.

I first learned the power of taking myself on a date in the early months of my divorce. I was new at being single, and discovering that I wasn't very good at it. Ever since I had started dating in my teen years, I had always been coupled up with someone. So being single was entirely new to me. And being single with kids? I was definitely not good at this.

As I told you in the beginning of this book, I lived with my parents in those early months, and spent a good portion of that time recovering from my failed marriage in a fetal position on the couch. But sometimes my parents would give me a night off from my depression by urging me to leave the house and do something for myself. Therefore, I'd go out.

Problem is, I was not very much fun to hang out with in my state of melancholy. I didn't want to burden any of my friends with my Eeyore attitude. I also didn't know what to do with myself. So I did the only thing I could think of.

I went to the bookstore.

The first several times I got a night to myself, this was where I always ended up. Here, I was surrounded by good friends. Anne Lamott, Alice Sebold, Maya Angelou, Liz Gilbert, Ernest Hemingway, Tim Farrington…. I loved the smell of the bookstore, the feel of books in my hands, the colorful covers, and the even more colorful stories. I'd grab a hot chocolate from the café, and then I'd spend the evening perusing the aisles until the store was ready to close.

Eventually, these dates with myself went to the next level. That's right folks, it was time for dinner and a movie.

On this special evening, I took myself out to an ethnic restaurant on the other side of town. I didn't even flinch when I told the waitress, "One, please." Inside, I was sure every eye was on me. But outwardly, I acted as if going out to eat by myself was no big thing.

Admittedly, it was a little awkward to sit at the table with no one in front of me. There was no one to talk to, or even to look at. I ate my dinner in silence, trying not to look around too much. I think I even brought a book to bide my time. Couples and families surrounded me, and it was apparent that I was the only single dining that night.

But you know what? As I ate, things started feeling a little less awkward. I realized I had somewhat of an advantage. I didn't have to make conversation if I didn't want to. I could fully enjoy my meal, focusing on each bite one at a time. No one was watching me. No one even cared that I was eating alone. I could order what I wanted, eat at my own pace, and just enjoy my own company.

After dinner, I walked next door to the movie theater and chose the movie I wanted to watch. Going by myself, I knew which movies it would *not* be—no action movies, no government schemes, no horror, no car chases. Without a date, I didn't have to worry about coordinating tastes at all in my movie choice.

"One for 'Garden State,' please," I told the person at the ticket counter.

Once inside and seated, couples surrounded me once again. But when the lights dimmed, it didn't matter. Even more, I realized just how awesome it is to go to the movies alone. I laughed aloud at the funny parts. And when things got sad, I cried without shame. There was no one there who would see my tears, so I had a really great therapy session right there in the middle of the movie theater. It was cathartic. It was liberating. And it was the best date I'd been on in my life.

Isn't it time you got some quality time with yourself? How about just straight-up pampering yourself, whether alone or not? There are so many things you can do. You could take yourself out for a healthy meal. You can go get a massage. You can play mini golf. You can…. Well, you can do one of these fifteen things, all under $20.

- Take a bubble bath with bath salts and scented candles.
- Enjoy a night in with a good book. Bonus if it includes a cozy drink and fuzzy socks.

- Take yourself out to lunch and a matinee.
- Buy yourself flowers. Throw in a small box of chocolates if you want to feel extra special.
- Purchase a new magazine and read it in the park.
- Get all Zen at a yoga class.
- Go for a bike ride in the country. Don't have a bike? Bike rentals are cheaper than you think.
- Check out the animals at the zoo.
- Learn something new at the museum.
- Be inspired at an art gallery.
- Visit with a friend you haven't seen in a while.
- Host a friend's night in.
- Be a tourist in your own town and check out the sights.
- Get more sleep. Sleep in, take a nap, or go to bed early.
- Make time for your significant other.

Now that you're feeling all gushy about yourself, it's time to commit. What I mean is to take a whole entire day off for yourself. If you can swing it, take a whole entire weekend.

My friend, Molly Kurland, is a successful massage therapist in the area we live, and the author of *Successful Strokes: A Realistic Guide to Creating a Lucrative Massage Business*. Her job as a masseuse demands a lot of her time and energy. Home life is no less energetic. Her family recently adopted two new puppies that have now reached the high-energy stage of teenagerhood. On top of that, Molly is working on writing and other creative endeavors. There just isn't much down time. So once a month, Molly kisses her family goodbye and heads for a weekend getaway in the nearby seaside town of Gualala. Here, there is no Internet, no TV, no phone calls, nothing. There's just her, a private room, a hot tub, and time to spend any way she wants. Sometimes she uses this free time just to read a good book. Sometimes it's when she gets her best writing in. Sometimes it's just a chance to breathe in silence. Molly has told me that this solo getaway is her key to happiness, and the way she ensures she can be fully present for her job and family when she's home. She's made it a priority to do this at least once a month.

We should all make it a priority to get away from it all on a regular basis. Just as I spelled out in chapters 1 and 4, it's so important to take a break from the busy part of life and just be still for a moment. It's especially important for our art so that we can unclutter our minds and create with an unencumbered soul. While taking a weekend away isn't possible for everyone, most of us are able to take a day off, maybe even a few hours.

After all, YOU are important. Now treat yourself that way.

CHALLENGE YOURSELF

Baby Step: It's time to write that list! Get out a pen and paper and write down all the things you're good at, the things about you that make you wonderful, and anything else that's positive about you. Enlist the help of your family and friends to make sure you have a complete list. Once you're done, hold on to that list. Then refer to it any time you feel doubt or criticism start to creep in.

Level Up: Take yourself out on a date—just you. Note how it feels to spend time by yourself in a crowd of people. Does it feel weird? Are there any benefits? Could you see yourself doing this more than just this once? Write about the experience when you're done.

Be Hardcore: Go away for the weekend. If that's too difficult, strive for just a day. But leave town by yourself so that you can spend some time getting to know YOU.

Chapter 6

Take a Soul Retreat

A few months ago, I found myself in a desperate place. I questioned everything in my life—my job, my writing, my health…everything. The walls were closing in on me, and it felt like there was nothing I could do. My soul was tapped out, dry, totally washed up. I felt like I was dying inside, and I didn't know how to escape feeling this way.

The moment of total despair wasn't just out of the blue. I had been on a slow and steady decline for months, probably even years. On the surface, I was unhappy with my work-life and the direction it was taking. For years, I had been headed toward my dream career at my job, and then, somehow, my path took a sharp right. I ended up in a position that looked nothing like what I had envisioned, and my soul was suffering because of it.

My desired solution was to quit my job and support my family with my books and writing. But since my art was not paying my bills, I needed my full-time job until the moment my art could support my life. Thing is, my art wasn't even close to supporting my life. So I needed my job to survive for the long-term. I began to resent the very thing that was putting food on my table, all because it was taking me away from the part of my life that I loved. Yes, my resentment was because my job wasn't the vision I had for my life. But the majority of my resentment was because it took up a huge portion of my day when I could be writing, and it sapped me of all my creative energy.

This is not an abnormal resentment. Of course I wanted to write full-time. And, of course I felt pulled when anything stood in the way. However, I had to work a full-time job to make ends meet, and my writing was going to have to fit in wherever I had empty spaces.

This brings me to a couple months ago. My job had become even more demanding. My stress level was through the roof. My creative life was practically non-existent as I fought to survive each day of my job without having a nervous breakdown. My eating habits were ridiculous as I used food as a coping mechanism. I felt like I had no purpose. I felt like there was no hope. I felt like this was just the way life was going to be, and I might as well give up any aspirations I had of being a full-time writer. There was no room for a creative life. I was ready to throw in the towel and just submit to being a worker for the rest of my life.

Thankfully, I recognized that this was not the answer. The answer was…I needed a break. That break came in the form of a one-day journey through the depths of my soul, and became the catalyst for this book you are reading right now. In this chapter, I not only want to share my experience of taking a soul retreat, I want to offer the necessary steps you can take if you, too, need to reboot your soul and regain footing on your creative path.

My Soul Retreat

It was a Thursday when I took a mental health day off work. I called in sick that morning because I was, in essence, very sick. I could barely breathe, and I couldn't fathom even going into the office that day. Everything felt daunting. There was no way I was going to be able to walk in there without quitting on the spot.

That morning, I waited until everyone had left the house, then I set to work planning my day. The very first thing I did was to figure out the exact areas of stress I wanted to tackle. This came down to three main topics— my job, my health, and my creative life. Then I mapped out three areas I could travel to so that I could meditate on each area of my life in a different place. Then I looked for words of wisdom about each issue. I found these words in the Bible, choosing passages that spoke directly to the problem I was facing. Once armed with all this, I was ready to begin.

I drove to the ocean first. Living near Bodega Bay, this is my go-to place for anytime I need to recharge. It was the perfect place to start my soul retreat and transition away from everything that was eating me up inside.

I set my coastal drive to the soundtrack of Sigur Ros, one of my favorite bands for getting out of my head and immersing myself in my retreat. Usually, it serves as my writing music. But on this day, it was my transition from a too-busy life to time with my spirit.

I was battling two overwhelming emotions on this drive: fear and hope. I was hopeful that I would find the answers I was looking for, and looking forward to this time I'd set aside to seek them. But I was fearful that I wouldn't find the answers. Even more, I was afraid I *would* find the answers, but they wouldn't be ones I was happy with.

There were tears on the drive, and it took almost the whole Sigur Ros album to get there. I found the exact portion of the coastline I'd envisioned, and pulled into a parking spot that faced the ocean. Then I let the album finish out as I stared out at the ocean, losing myself to the vastness of the sea.

When ready, I came out of the car and found a spot on a picnic bench. I brought with me a box of Kleenex (which I had to buy on the way there since I'd forgotten!), and my journal. Then, as I watched the waves crash against the rocks below, I began my soul retreat.

At first I just stared at the ocean, allowing the water to guide me from my overworked mind to utter and complete quiet. I cleared my thoughts, focusing on nothing more than the waves churning below the bluff I was sitting on, and letting go of every thought that was trying to invade my time of peace. Once my shoulders were able to relax and my breathing became slow and steady, I turned to the words I had chosen for myself that morning. I read the first one, and then the second. And that's when I was interrupted.

"Pay attention."

I heard these words like a whisper inside of me. They were soft in volume and loud in intention, and they were unmistakably *for me*. Their meaning couldn't be more clear.

What do you see? What do you hear?

I put the words I was reading down, and then I looked back out at the ocean in front of me, searching beyond the churning waves to find the message.

The first thing I noticed was a seagull sitting on a rock as the ocean swirled all around it. Each time the wave crashed, the seagull would flinch, but not move away.

Second, I saw a black bird floating just out of reach from the tumultuous part of the ocean. The waves kept stretching toward that bird, but the bird seemed to hold no fear as it kept diving underwater to find food.

Third, I heard a loud boom each time the waves crashed against the rocks, and then saw the rainbow in the spray as the water flew up into the air before landing back in the ocean.

Fourth, I noticed how large this expanse of the sea was, realizing it was only a small fraction of the whole sea, the whole world, the whole universe. And I was right there, smaller than all of them. And the problem I was grappling with? It was even smaller than that.

Here's what I figured out from these four things:

1. Seagull: In that moment, I was the seagull, and the waves were my job. I had danger all around me that was making me feel uncomfortable. Yet, instead of doing anything about it, I was staying near it as a victim of my circumstances. I was keeping myself in fear instead of just moving out of the way.

2. Black bird: The black bird was what I wanted to be—someone who took risks in my quest for security, but didn't let fear be the ruler. These risks might include getting a new job, learning a new skill, public speaking, marketing myself, taking smart financial risks, or anything else that would keep me from getting too comfortable in any one situation. The danger might be all around, but I'd be moving alongside it to survive, and be proactive so as to not be swept away. I'd be in control while utilizing the very source of danger to my advantage.

3. Ocean spray: This is the one of the most dangerous parts of the ocean. Anything that gets caught in the crashing waves will be smashed against the rocks. And yet, the rainbow exists in each large wave of spray. Something so beautiful in something so deadly. In the Christian faith, the rainbow serves as God's promise. I took that vision of the rainbow as a sign that through it all, God will provide. He has not deserted me. I'm going to get beat up. I will fall.

I will fail many times. But I am not alone in this journey. Life, despair, jobs, sickness, health, richness, poverty.... None of that is bigger than God, and He will be with me every step of the way.

4. The vastness of the ocean: God is bigger than my problems. I realized that I kept forgetting that. I kept treating my problem as if it were the biggest thing in the world, even the universe. But the biggest truth is, it's not. My Creator is.

This is just what I discovered in my first session of meditation and reflection. The following two sessions were just as impactful. I found solutions to the issues that had been plaguing me—real answers that I could act upon easily.

To be clear, this day of reflection, my own personal soul retreat, became a day that changed my life forever. Before I took this day off, I was floundering and felt hopeless. After my soul retreat, I gained a sense of clarity that wouldn't have been possible before. I gained tools I was able to take with me and use any time I felt like the world was caving in again.

This is what I want for you. I want you to be able to clearly see the path you're supposed to be on, and the steps you need to take to get to your desired destination. I want you to let go of some, if not all, of those burdens that have been weighing you down and keeping you from your art. I want you to hear whispered answers to the issues you are facing, and I want you to learn how to make those answers a reality.

I want you to take a soul retreat.

Taking a Soul Retreat

Through the past several chapters, I've already taught you everything you need to know to take a soul retreat. But now, we are going to put it all together.

The first thing you need to do is to decide the WHAT. What is weighing you down? What is tearing you apart? What is paralyzing you? Make a list, and don't be shy about it. Write down everything you can think of. Then look over that list. Are there any noticeable themes? Can you combine any issues? Pare that list down and then look it over again. Do any issues stand out more than others? Choose no more than three, and let those be your focus. Don't worry about the issues you're leaving behind. You can always address those later. But for this exercise, I only want you to choose three or less. Any more than that, and you may become too overwhelmed to tackle anything on that list.

Next, I want you to search out words of wisdom that address each one of your issues, just like we did in Chapter 4. If you can't find any of your own, you can choose any words of wisdom I've included at crissilangwell.com/free-resources-for-creative-souls. Choose at least three quotes, lyrics, spiritual messages, etc. Don't think them over too much right now, but do include them if they touch you in some way.

Third, map out locations where you can find uninterrupted solace to reflect on each of your issues. I recommend finding a new place for each issue, just to keep each one separate from the other issues. But even one special place is enough. It can be the ocean, the forest, a park, or whatever. It just needs to be a place that is A) away from home, and B) a place where no one or thing will impede your ability to detach.

Finally, I want you to find a day when you can completely clear your schedule. Leave the kids with a sitter. Take a day off work. Assign your normal tasks to someone else.

I know that what I'm asking of you is not that simple. I know that for some of you, taking a whole day off is next to impossible. But I'm begging you, do this for yourself. YOU ARE WORTH IT. You owe it to yourself and your craft to regain everything you've misplaced by living such a busy life. The world will not fall apart without you for one day. Your kids will not starve to death if you're not the one feeding them. Your job will not go under if you don't come in for one day.

And that's all this is—one day.

This one day will not only make you a better artist, it will make you a better parent, a better worker, a better friend, and a better human being.

This one day will expand your soul.

Putting it in Action

The day of your soul retreat can feel a little nerve-wracking. You will feel a range of emotions—silliness over making such a big deal about this, fear that nothing will come of it, apprehension that any answers you might receive won't be the ones you want, anxiety that you might miss the answers completely.... Let yourself feel. If you need to cry, then cry. If you need to yell about it, then yell. Release those feelings. And then, let those feelings go.

Pack or prepare the following items for your day:

- Kleenex!
- A full tank of gas if you're driving
- A journal
- A plan
- What you want to address
- Words of wisdom
- Schedule of events
- Destination(s)
- Food and water (don't let thirst or hunger get in your way of connecting with your soul)
- A blanket or chair, or something comfy to sit on
- Inspirational music
- An open mind

Now that you're prepared and your schedule is clear, make your way to your first (or only) destination. Let this journey be a part of your retreat. I encourage you to listen to music that inspires you. Or, you may want to just keep the music off so that you can start to quiet your spirit.

Once you are ready, follow these guidelines for every single issue:

1. Arrive at your destination
2. Be still for a little while and transition into your retreat
3. Read wisdom and meditate on the words (contemplative reading)
4. Pray/focus on wisdom and the issue at hand
5. Be still and remain open for answers
6. Journal
7. Offer a prayer of gratitude

Each one of these steps are equally important. Be still, then practice Lectio Divina, or contemplative reading, just as we learned in Chapter 4. If you are a praying person, set the words aside and pray. If not, just meditate on the issue at hand, merged with the words of wisdom about this particular issue. Then, be still once again. Keep an open mind and an open heart for any answers you may receive from God or The Universe. Watch and listen to your surroundings. Let the answers come to you, spoken through whatever is around you. Be patient.

When the moment is right (and only you will know), pick up your journal and start writing. If you still haven't received an answer, this might be when it happens. Write down everything you are feeling and experiencing— partially to attach this day to your memory, and partially to become even clearer about your experience.

Finally, offer a prayer of thanks to God or The Universe. Do this even if you still have not received an answer.

Let's say that's the case—you've done everything you're supposed to do in a soul retreat, and you feel like your issue is left unresolved. There are two reasons why this might be. One, it's not the right time for this issue to be solved. Or two, you're not ready to receive the answer.

If you have gone through a whole soul retreat and are still burdened without any kind of solution, it just means that you have more work to do. It may take a few soul retreats for you to become complete with whatever is weighing you down. It will come. But your level of patience and grace are needed more than anything.

CHALLENGE YOURSELF

Be Hardcore: The challenge for this chapter is the same for everyone: Take a soul retreat. If you picked up this book, it's because something is hindering you from reaching your creative soul. You need a soul retreat to find out what that something is, and to learn how to manage it so that you can regain your creativity.

Would you like to share what happened on your soul retreat? Email me at crissi@crissilangwell.com, and put "Creative Soul Retreat" in the subject line.

Extra credit: I wrote more on my soul retreat in my blog. Go to crissilangwell.com/category/soul-talk and read Soul Retreats 1 & 2. For extra reading, also read the Children's Bell Tower.

Section 3

Organization

In a perfect world, we could focus on art at all moments of the day. However, we live in the real world. You have to go to work. You have to put food on the table. You have a family to take care of, or even just yourself. There are responsibilities you must attend to so that you don't end up on the streets. And somehow, you need to balance all of that with your art and wellbeing.

The next five chapters are the meat of this book. This section offers tips on organizing your full-time life through managing your money, time, and priorities. I also share ways to keep the space around you organized, and how to make time for your health. The knowledge you gain from these chapters will not only add order to your life, but you will free up a considerable amount of time and mind space so that you can focus on your craft.

Chapter 7

Managing Your Money

There's a reason why the term "starving artist" is so popular. Hardly anyone wakes up one day, decides to create art, and becomes instantly rich and famous from their creations. The reality is that your art will not make you money in those first few years. There's even a possibility that it will never make you a significant amount of money, and you will have to learn how to balance your art with other ways to support yourself until you retire.

Why are we trying to be artists then? Oh yeah, because we love this as much as we love breathing.

If you're still reading this after figuring out that art is not a get rich quick scheme (shocker!), then I have good news for you—you don't necessarily have to be starving to be an artist. You just need to learn how to manage your money better. Not only will this allow more of your hard-earned income to land in your pocket, but it will also free you from a good amount of stress you're probably feeling that is standing in the way of true creativity.

Money is a passionate subject for me, mostly because there was a time when I had none. I know what it's like to be days away from payday, and wonder how I'm going to make a can of beans and crackers stretch until then. I know what it's like to have the electricity shut off and no money to turn it back on. I know what it's like to depend on government aid to be able to feed my family and stretch my meager income. I know what it's like to live without.

Through hard work and diligence, I was able to escape the clutches of poverty. I started working at the newspaper, and my income grew. I met my husband and we eventually moved in together, doubling our income in the process. I was able to build up my non-existent credit through a couple of low-balance credit cards. Financially, life was most definitely looking up.

Of course, more money, more problems, right?

With a larger paycheck and more credit, I suffered amnesia about what it was like to live a simple lifestyle. My expenses grew faster than my income, and credit became my crutch. While I lived in poverty, I had no debt. But out of poverty, my bills included hundreds of dollars that I was paying each month to credit cards. Not only did our wedding and extra book costs end up on credit cards, but so did some of our simple living costs. If I didn't have money for something, I used my credit card to get through. After all, the minimum payments would only rise a few dollars, right?

Wrong.

It's amazing how fast credit card debt can increase when you're not careful. I remember looking at the amount of money I was spending each month and feeling disgusted when I saw much of my paycheck was going toward credit cards. There I was, making more money than I ever had in my life, and I still felt that same dread about money that I did in my days of poverty. I was caught in a never-ending money cycle—pay all the minimum payments for my credit cards, have too little left over after bills, use credit cards to make ends meet, repeat.

Around this time, my husband and I signed up for a money management course called Financial Peace University. I still had a lot of pride about money, and I was sure that there was nothing this course was going to teach me that I didn't already know. After all, I spent years living on a meager budget and living without credit. I figured this would just be a simple brush-up, since I was already an expert on budgeting.

Because, you know, my debt proved how well I handled money, right?

It became clear how little I actually knew about money. The lessons I learned shaped a new way to handle my money. It allowed me to reconfigure my bills so that I could break free from living paycheck to paycheck. I'm happy to say that I no longer have credit card debt, and I now have money left over for fun things, like taking the whole family to Hawaii over the summer.

Wouldn't it be wonderful to never be burdened by money again? Think about how good it would feel to devote your time to your art without worrying about whether it's going to pay the bills or not.

The truth about money stress is that it tends to overwhelm every single aspect of your life. While it's true that money can't buy you happiness, living in debt can make you miserable. It hinders the creative process, fills your life with fear, and can send you into a pit that feels impossible to escape. Society has taught us that living in debt is normal. We've come to believe that credit is a way of life. We have become slaves to our money, and we're okay with this. We're told that buying things we can't afford will make us happy. But where is this happiness when it's time to pay the bill?

I am not a rich person in the least. However, I suffer very little stress when it comes to money. The financial course my husband and I took revealed so much to both of us about money, alleviating us from a lot of needless stress.

I want this for you, as well. So with the financial wisdom I gained from this course, along with living this wisdom in real life, here are four steps you can do right now that will free you from a lot of worry in regards to finances.

1. Make a list of all your expenses
Before you do anything, create a list of everything you spend in a month. Don't leave anything out. Include

regular bills, debt bills, food costs, money spent on entertainment, clothing expenses, and anything else you regularly spend money on throughout the month. If an expense varies, write down the average amount you would spend on that item. Be honest in this process. You are the only one seeing this list, and any discrepancies will only make it harder to gain the upper hand with your money.

Once all you have listed all your expenses, place them in one of four groups: primary living, secondary living, debt, and extra.

Primary living expenses will include things like your rent, food costs, utility bills, and any other bill that is vital to your life.

Secondary living expenses will include bills that you need to pay, but won't impede your quality of life if you don't have it. For example, this could include things like gas money or car payment and insurance (since you could take the bus), or your cell phone or Internet bill (since shutting it off would be an inconvenience, but you're not going to die).

Debt includes bills that you can eventually pay down to a zero balance. This expense list will include your mortgage, car payment, credit card bills, and student loans.

Your extra expenses will include items like beauty (hair care, makeup), gym membership, clothing costs, entertainment costs, gift-giving costs, and vacation costs.

Once you feel like you've itemized every one of your expenses under these four groups, scrutinize it even further. Are there costs you've included in your primary living expenses that could actually go under secondary living expenses? Are there secondary living expenses you could classify as an extra cost, instead? Prioritize the items of each group until you are satisfied with the complete list.

2. Create a budget

Here's where this list is going to come in handy. Create an excel spreadsheet that lists every single one of your expenses. I've created a handy one that you can access at crissilangwell.com/free-resources-for-creative-souls to help you get started. On your budget list, write the expenses in order of the groups I had you list in the first step: Primary living, secondary living, debt, and extra. Now that you've done that, there are a few more expenses I want you to add to your budget: an allowance of pocket money, and an emergency savings fund. The pocket money is yours to spend as you like. But remember, when it's gone, it's gone. You do not get to borrow from other funds if you've used up all your pocket money. The emergency fund is for all those expenses you weren't expecting. These are the things you would normally grab your credit card to pay for—a new car transmission, your dog's broken leg, a chipped tooth, a new washer…. Ideally, this fund will hold $1,000, but don't let that number scare you. With a strict plan in place, you are perfectly capable of saving enough to cover emergencies (just a side note: please be clear on what an emergency is NOT. For example, a night out on the town or a new outfit is NOT an emergency).

Next, pay attention to the grand total of these expenses. How does it line up with your income? Are the expenses less than what you bring in every month? Great! You're in the minority! Put that extra income to use by adding it to your savings. For the rest of us, we have some work to do.

One of the biggest stresses about money is that we often feel managed by it. With a budget, you are essentially taking back that power. You make the money, so why is your money controlling you? Tell your money where to go, as Dave Ramsey, the creator of Financial Peace University, often says.

Your goal is to create what's called a zero-based budget. This is where your expenses and income will cancel each other out completely so that the total equals zero.

I understand this is kind of a terrifying concept. The first time I heard about zero-based budgeting, I wanted to take my paycheck and run. *Are you telling me that I can't have any of the money I just earned?* Thankfully, that's not what it means at all. It does mean, however, that you are going to need to budget your extra money instead of just spending whatever you have left over.

Now that you have your expenses listed and see that they equal more than your income, seek out areas where you can trim. I recognize this isn't easy. You are going to have to sacrifice a little to ensure you aren't spending more than you make. First, look for the things you can give up easily. Can you live without eating out? Can you let go of your Starbucks obsession? Can you decrease the amount you are spending on clothing? Is your food budget too high?

If your expenses are still more than your income after you've trimmed all the extra costs, you are going to have to dig deeper. If there's nothing left on your list of extras that can be reduced or deleted, you are going to have to start scrutinizing your secondary living expenses. Can you reduce the services on your cell phone? Can you live without television and/or Internet? Can you start taking the bus instead of driving, at least until your finances are more manageable?

Or the extreme—can you sell any of your belongings to reduce any of your debt? Can you sell your car and take the bus permanently? Can you hold a garage sale? Can you put a few items on Craigslist that you no longer use?

You may need to make some hard choices, and it won't be comfortable. But these sacrifices are only until your debt is paid down and your budget is much more manageable.

When you have your budget zeroed out, you can move on to the next step: reducing your debt. Warning, the budget you just created is going to continue to change.

3. Dancing the debt snowball.

Have you ever been to a snowball dance? This is when one couple starts out on the dance floor. As soon as the music stops, they separate and find new partners to dance with, thus inviting two more people on the floor. The music stops again, and then those four people will find four new people to dance with.

In a way, this is the dance we are going to do with your debt.

Glance over the debt you have listed on your budget, and order these items by the amount you owe. The first item will be your largest, which will probably be your mortgage if you own your house. Next is probably your student loan or your car payment. Next are your larger credit cards, followed by your store credit cards. And so on. Now I'm going to give you some advice that might seem controversial: pay only the minimum payments on every single bit of your debt, except for the smallest debt you owe. I know this seems totally backwards, but trust me on this.

Note: If you are already paying only the minimum payment on every single bit of debt you owe, you are going to have to adjust your budget one more time so that you can pay more on that smallest bit of debt.

The idea behind this method is to get that smallest debt completely paid off as quick as possible. This means you need to throw as much money as it as you can until it no longer exists. Once you've done that, pat yourself on the back! You officially have less debt!

But don't stop there.

Take that amount you were spending to that first bit of debt, and apply it to the next smallest debt. Pay that amount until you have erased that debt. Then repeat. As you continue to pay off debt, the amount you can pay on that lowest bit of debt will get larger and larger—like a snowball. However, you won't be spending more of your income to do so. As each debt is paid off, the process of eliminating debt gets faster and more satisfying.

For example, let's say you have three credit cards. The first has a balance of $8,000. The second has a balance of $5,000. And the third has a balance of $2,000. You have been paying $200 to each of them a month to try and pay them off, which is more than the minimum payment. For this example's sake, we'll just say the minimum payment on each is $150. To follow this step, start making $150 payments to the credit cards with the largest amount of debt, and then take that extra money and apply it to the smaller debt. With $50 extra from the first two cards, you can now make $300 payments to the smallest debt. In less than seven months, that smallest debt will be completely paid off. Once that happens, apply that $300 payment to the next credit card. So instead of paying $150 to take care of that $5,000 debt, you will now be making $450 payments, and will pay it off in a little over eleven months. Finally, apply that $450 to the $150 you are paying on the $8,000 debt, making it a $600 payment. In just over thirteen months, that debt will be wiped out.

In our example scenario, we took $15,000 of debt and paid it off in two and a half years. Do you see how easy that was? And do you see how much money you will be able to put to better use once your credit card debt is wiped out?

Finally, make a vow to never take on debt again, especially through credit cards! If you don't have the money saved for it, you can't have it. End of story. To ensure you never use a credit card again, I encourage you to cut up each card, and then cancel the card as soon as it's paid off.

4. Save $ for the big things

Earlier in this chapter, I mentioned our family trip to Hawaii. Years ago, a trip like this would never have happened unless we financed the whole thing using credit cards. A week in the tropics would end up being years of debt while we tried to pay it off.

I'll have you know that this past summer, we flew our family of five to Hawaii, stayed in a penthouse suite, ate out for many meals, enjoyed a few excursions, and came home without adding any amount of debt to our expenses, even though the vacation cost around $6,000. We paid cash for the whole vacation, and even came home with a few extra dollars.

So how did we do this? The obvious answer is that we saved up for it. But it only took six months for us to do so. We budgeted an amount that was easy for us to put aside each month, and then worked backwards from there to decide how long it would take to save the full amount. We budgeted our vacation much like we budget our monthly expenses: we figured out where we wanted to go, the cost of airline tickets, where we wanted to stay, the activities we wanted to enjoy, and the cost of food, including groceries and eating out. We even budgeted an amount for souvenirs. Once that figure was established, we could pick a date for the vacation, factoring in how much we could save each month and how long it would take us to save.

It feels wonderful to enjoy a vacation when you don't have to worry about the bill afterwards. We were able to completely detach from our lives at home and enjoy a week of relaxation. We could spend money freely (the first time in a long time!) because we had planned it that way.

What made this experience even sweeter was the contrast our vacation spending held to our spending habits at home. For one week, we were able to live without strict money rules (at least inside of what we had planned).

Think about it this way. If you have dessert every single night after dinner, it becomes less special. Sure, it still tastes good. But it becomes an expected part of the meal. However, if you save dessert for special occasions, it suddenly tastes so much more delicious. The same goes for money. If you spend frivolously all the time, it just doesn't hold that same feeling of pleasure. You have to spend more and more to be able to gain that high you get from gaining something new. But if you stick to a budget and refrain from treating yourself, it feels that much more special when you *are* able to indulge (and especially because you have planned for it!).

If there's something you want and you don't have the money for it, you need to really search your soul about whether you *need* it, or if you just want it on impulse. If you really want it, you can have it. But you need to plan for it.

Let's say you want a new computer. Check the price for the model you want, and then coordinate the money you can put toward it with when you want it purchased. If you want it sooner than your income will allow, you may need to adjust your budget a little more to make that happen. If that's not possible, you're just going to have to accept that your computer ownership days will be later than you want.

Finally, save for the not-so-fun expenses, as well. As I mentioned in step #2, you'll want to set aside a little bit each paycheck to go toward things like car repairs or expensive health issues. I can't stress this enough. If your car transmission goes out, or your dentist visit doesn't go so well, you'll rest much easier knowing that you have the funds to cover these expenses.

To wrap things up, I want to make a couple of points very clear. Living by a strict budget is going to take time. Don't beat yourself up if, for the first few months, you go over your budget or end up using your credit card. It may be because your budget needs to be worked at a little more until it's manageable. Or it could be because old habits are hard to break. Be gentle with yourself. And be patient waiting for the results.

Next, recognize where your satisfaction is coming from now. Before, you may have experienced feelings of happiness from gaining new things. While living on a budget isn't nearly as shiny and exciting, doesn't it feel good to be the boss of where your money is going? Don't discount that satisfaction of being in control of your cash flow.

Third, and the reason we are even talking about money in a book on creativity: how is that mental block going? The desperation that comes with money issues can affect your art in a real way. Your creations could take on the odor of that desperation. You might be prone to sell out, being untrue to your creative desires just to make a buck. Or worse, you may decide to give up your art altogether because it isn't making you the money you need.

If you can manage your income and limit your expenses, you will experience freedom with your art, and will find it easier to create for the sake of creating, instead of as a means to an end.

And isn't that why we became artists in the first place?

CHALLENGE YOURSELF

Baby Step: I want you to create your own budget. As I referenced before, I have created a spreadsheet to get you started, which you can access at crissilangwell.com/free-resources-for-creative-souls. It's nothing fancy, but it's what I refer to with every single paycheck to ensure I'm living within my means.

Level Up: Reduce your debt by creating a debt snowball. Outside of your mortgage, set a date for when you can be completely debt free!

Be Hardcore: Take a Financial Peace University course. I receive no financial gain whatsoever by referring you to this course. However, I believe in it so much, I think everyone should take it. To find a course near you, visit www.daveramsey.com/fpu and search for a nearby location. These courses are Christian-based and are generally held in churches. Nonetheless, the course tries to keep religious talk to a minimum. People of many faiths, and a few of no faith at all, attended the course my husband and I took. Financial Peace University helped all of us to gain a much better handle on our money and live without financial stress.

Chapter 8

Managing Your Time

We live in a busy world. Thanks to technology, we have the ability to connect with anyone at any time. We have hundreds of ways to avoid boredom right at our fingertips. Wisdom is just a click of a button away, either through a simple search for answers or through an elaborate how-to video. These are exciting times to live in.

These are also the most distracting times.

Your undivided focus is vital to the art you are creating. This, of course, makes you completely susceptible to anything at any given time that is competing for your attention. These distractions may come in the form of well-meaning friends, a scroll through social media, something interesting on TV, or just simply checking your email. If you're not careful, the time you have set aside for your art can be consumed by these distractions.

Your time is important. And if you are dividing your time between your art, a full-time job, raising a family, and the many other arenas of your life, you don't have much time to waste.

Or, perhaps you feel like you have no time left for your art.

I want to pause here and acknowledge that your time is different from my time, and the time of everyone else who is reading this book. I do not know your circumstance, and I cannot dictate how you spend your time in your life. Some of you who will be able to uncover a few extra hours for your art after reading this chapter. And some of you may only be able to uncover a few minutes. Different priorities require different responses. For example, you may have very little wiggle room if you have a full-time job or are raising a family. However, I'm certain you can amend the time you spend perusing social media or watching TV.

I also want to remind you that there is a season for everything. Parents of young children probably feel more than frustrated about the lack of time left over for their creative endeavors. However, children don't stay young forever. Eventually they become more independent, and require less of your devoted attention. Same with your job. You may be frustrated because you are working so hard at making someone else money, when you really want to be devoting your time to your art. Your time will come. You may only have an hour or so a day to give to your art, and are a slave to your cubicle for the rest of the day. This makes that one hour so much more valuable. But if you keep at it, using that hour as best as you can, the day may come when you can decrease the amount of hours you spend working for someone else, and increase the amount of time you spend creating.

Before we go any further, I want to remind you that I am one of you. As you read in the introduction of this book, I have very little room for fooling around. I have a full-time job. I volunteer with my writing club. I am training as a leader with my church. I am raising a blended family of teenagers. I am a human being. I am busier than I ever have been in my life. And in the past several years, I have produced a half dozen novels, regularly churning out one to two novels a year.

I know what it feels like to be busy. But I have also learned how to find pockets of time for my art, and make the most of that time. In this chapter, I want to teach you what I have learned over the years so that you can be even more productive when it comes to your craft.

The easiest way to find extra time is to take an inventory of how you spend each day, and see which areas you can cut. You are going to have to make some sacrifices. You are going to have to say "no" more. You may need to reduce the amount of time you spend socializing with your friends.

Some cuts are going to be easier than others. Some might be extremely difficult. For example, you might need to let go of a volunteer position or a few social "obligations." I recognize that you might feel that these areas require your involvement. But is the time you are spending in these areas more important than the time you need for your art? Only you can answer this question.

If you keep a calendar (and I suggest you do), how busy does it look right now? Can you cancel any events you have planned? Are there activities you can cut back on? Before you commit to anything, think about WHY you are committing. Is your attendance required? Does this commitment add to your life? When anyone asks you to take part in something new, think long and hard before you agree. Be slow to say "yes." Understand that every time you say "yes" to something, you are saying "no" to something else—including the time you spend on your craft.

Another easy way to find time is to avoid the things that are wasting your time. I am specifically talking about television, social media, your email, and the Internet in general. It's too easy to get sucked into these different areas, wasting precious time you could be spending on your art. If you need to, schedule some time when you can devote your attention to these things. But mindlessly checking your email several times a day, or even just submitting to the distractions of what other people are posting to Facebook, is not a good use of your time at all.

You only have twenty-four hours in day. Do not let insignificant distractions take up significant portions of that time.

To create time for your art, you may need to sacrifice some of your sleep. Now, I'm not saying to give up sleep altogether, or to sleep less than what's healthy. Your creativity depends on how much rest you get. However, you can still be well rested and wake up an hour or two earlier than your normal wake up time.

Personally, my favorite time for writing is in those two hours before everyone in my house wakes up. In the 5 o'clock hour, the house is quiet and there are very little distractions. It's the time I have gifted myself to ensure I always have time for my books, and that nothing else will take that away from me. Plus, I have a sense of accomplishment when I am able to write first thing in the morning.

I highly encourage you to wake up early every day to work on your art. This might mean you need to start going to bed earlier to make this happen. If you're more of a night owl, you can, of course, work on your art late at night. However, my argument for working first thing in the morning is that it ensures you are able to devote time to your craft every single day. If you work at night, you run the risk of something getting in the way, or that you will lose motivation by the end of the day.

Finding time for your art might mean you need to steal small pockets of time to get it done. If you work full-time, you might consider sacrificing your lunch break for a half hour of creativity. If you're a full-time parent, utilize your child's naptime for your craft (that is, if you don't need some necessary rest, yourself!). You may only have time to create an outline of what you plan to do. What you create might even feel insignificant. Just know this, even a little bit of work each day adds up to a finished project sometime in the future.

When deciding how to spend your time, consider quality over quantity. Nix all parties and social events, but schedule time to spend with a close friend. Forgo a large promotion at work in favor of time spent with your family. Give up a night watching TV on the couch for an intimate evening out with your spouse. Just because you are trying to create time for your art does not mean you need to stop enjoying life. You just need to make sure that you are filling your time with soul enriching activities instead of mindless time sucks.

Create a set-in-stone schedule for your art. Block out a certain amount of time each day, and then protect that time as if your life depends on it. In a way, it does. This is the time when you and your soul get to come together to create something beautiful, raw, and full of life. If you don't take that seriously, how do you expect anyone else to? Give your time as much priority as you would your job or an event you agreed to attend. Isn't your craft just as important? Do not treat your creativity as a mere hobby, or as anything less than significant. You were called to create. It is your duty to create. So do your part by limiting your distractions and letting those around you know that you are unavailable for the number of hours you have set aside for your art. Turn off your phone. Avoid the Internet. Close and lock the door. Leave your house, if you have to. This is *your* time. Make the most of it.

Finally, be realistic about what you are capable of doing in a day. One of the biggest ways to feel like a failure is to overstate what you would like to accomplish within a set amount of hours. You are not a superhuman. You may be capable of creating gorgeous things within your creativity, but you are still a mere mortal. *Let yourself be mortal.* Some days you will be more productive. Some days you won't be able to accomplish much of anything. And some days you need more rest than art. Allow for some downtime to recharge. If you get yourself on a schedule that allows for art every day, consider skipping a day now and then just to relax and refresh your soul.

Time is what we make of it. So make the most of your time.

CHALLENGE YOURSELF

Baby Step: If you're not already keeping a calendar, go out right now and buy a day planner. Write down all of your commitments, and then see if there's anything you can do to free up some of your time. Be sure to schedule in time when you can work on your art!

Level Up: Free yourself from distractions for a full twenty-four hours by keeping the TV and Internet off for one whole day. Each time you feel tempted to cheat, remind yourself that this is only one day, and you can have these distractions back tomorrow. Journal on how your day went at the end of the day.

Be Hardcore: Prohibit all time wasters for one week. This means saying "no" to TV, going out to the movies, and mindlessly perusing the Internet. Schedule the times you will check your email, and stick to that schedule. Decline any invitations to events. Wake up an hour earlier than usual. Pay attention to the amount of time you have gained each day. Then journal how this week has changed your perception of the time you have.

Chapter 9

Being the A-Lister

Can I confess something to you? Organization is not my natural strong suit. I'm actually quite scattered. I can do a week's worth of laundry in a day, fold it all up, and then place it in the laundry basket. But that last step of putting clothes away is just too much. I'll resort to living out of that laundry basket for the rest of the week, shoving aside the folded clothes on top to get to the ones on the bottom. In just a few days, all that hard work will have gone to waste because I just couldn't find it in me to put the clothes in a drawer or hang them in the closet.

This seems to be a running theme, as I rarely put things back in their proper spot. As a result, I misplace so many of my belongings. I've even gone so far as to put something down in the wrong spot and look at it, knowing that I'm going to lose it if I leave it there. But some little voice inside me will say that this time it will be different, and I actually believe it—until I can't remember where I put that very same object.

It doesn't stop there. I'm terrible at being on time. I forget people's names as soon as they tell them to me. I won't remember the first instruction given to me by the time I hear the third step. I have gotten lost in my own neighborhood. I am easily distracted. If I'm interrupted, it takes me at least ten minutes to remember what I was doing in the first place. Sidetrack is my middle name....

It's easy for us creative types to be a bit scattered. Our brains don't function on a straight line, but tend to travel as inspiration moves us. This is definitely true for me. I also attribute my cluttered mind to being so incredibly busy, I just don't have room to remember every single detail.

To compensate for my scattered mind, I've come to rely heavily on writing everything down in the form of lists. I carry a notebook with me at all times, and use it to record everything, from things I need to accomplish to mapping out a particular stress I need to work on. If someone calls me, even just for a social call, I will grab a notepad and have it ready in case I need to write anything down. I know my mind. If I'm told anything I will need to remember later, I have to write it down or I will forget it as soon as I hang up the phone.

Keeping lists has also been a way for me to organize the thoughts and worries I have rolling around my head. A few weeks ago, I was feeling really overwhelmed because I had taken on more projects than I knew what to do with. I was doing some freelance work for three different authors. At the same time, I was trying to wrap up the final stages of a book I was getting ready to release. In addition, I was amped to continue writing this book you're reading now. It all felt like too much, too fast. I kept going over all of these jobs, taking turns to stress over each one in a never-ending cycle of anxiety. There were no solutions, just stress. I was getting nowhere.

This is when I grabbed the nearest notebook, which happened to be my journal. I opened it up and just started scribbling down everything that came to my mind. If I thought it, I wrote it. Then, when the page was completely marked up, I began organizing my thoughts into a plan. I mapped out my entire week, dictating when I would start and finish certain tasks so I could finish each project on time. By the time I was done, I had a manageable to-do list, and my anxiety was gone.

I think what helped me to alleviate my stress the most was to see every single one of my worries in front of me. When they were just rolling around in my head, I had no way of gauging how big or how small each one was. To me, they seemed enormous, and definitely unmanageable. But when I wrote them down, I was able to see the reality of the situation instead of just guessing about how bad things were. My list served as an inventory of my thoughts and worries, allowing me to prioritize each item by level of difficulty and importance. For example, one job I was sure would take at least half a day was finished in only twenty minutes.

With my list, I was able to disprove the lies I had created about all I had to do. I was able to organize my cluttered mind and make order in my busy, busy world.

If you also classify yourself as being scattered, I highly recommend that you get in the habit of making lists. This starts with the dreaded to-do list.

Now, don't zone out on me here, because this is important. This is not some honey-do list of things you don't want to do, nor is it a way to ruin a perfectly good Saturday. Keeping a to-do list can actually be a great thing. It will help you to organize your time much better, ultimately giving you more time to work with. And it will help to relieve some of your worry since you don't have to remember what you need to do—the list will do that for you. Having a to-do list will offer you a clear visual of everything that's required of you, dispelling any untruths about how overly busy you are.

List your Week

I tend to create a weekly to-do list first, and then break it down in days. The most important part about creating a list like this is to be realistic about what I can accomplish in any given amount of time. I usually load up my schedule with tasks I hope to accomplish. But I allow myself wiggle room by the end of the week so that I have time to play catchup with all I wasn't able to finish.

With your to-do list, however, understand the difference between being busy and being productive. If you find that your list is filled with many unimportant tasks that are getting you nowhere, it's time for you to prioritize what really needs to be done, and what can be erased off the list.

List your Meals

Another list every household should keep is a grocery shopping list. But I'm going to take this one step further. Before you create a list of groceries for the week, you need to create a menu of what you will be making for dinner.

A weekly meal plan has been a lifesaver for our busy household. It takes away the guesswork when it comes time to make dinner. The kids no longer ask what's for dinner, they just refer to the menu. And it's vital to creating a proper grocery shopping list with everything we need for the week. Otherwise, we're left to scour the cabinets, trying to find inspiration from a smorgasbord of ingredients we don't really feel like cooking. With a meal plan, we can get as creative as we want, knowing that we can just buy all the ingredients at the store.

You should never go shopping without a grocery list. Without a plan in place, you're liable to spend too much on impulse purchases. You are also prone to forgetting things you actually do need. If you don't have a list, you'll likely spend much more time in the store, and you will definitely spend more money. A grocery shopping list ensures that you are much more efficient on your shopping trip, and you won't blow your entire paycheck on food.

To help you with creating your own menu and grocery shopping lists, I've made a 30-day menu of meals, plus a corresponding shopping list. You can access it at crissilangwell.com/free-resources-for-creative-souls.

List your Finances

Lists are also a good idea when it comes to your expenses. I know we went over budgeting last chapter, but that doesn't mean managing your money will never be an issue. Raising three teenagers, I know all too well what it's like to be handed a piece of paper from school or sports with requests for money. As much as I plan for those kinds of costs, it's always more than I bargained for.

When you find yourself facing a bunch of unplanned expenses, the best thing you can do is to make a list of those expenses. If you don't, you'll just end up wallowing in misery over how broke you feel. By listing your expenses, you are giving yourself a clearer picture about how much you really need to pay. More than likely, it's not even as bad as you think it is. With your finances laid out in list form in front of you, it will be easier to figure out how much you need to buckle down to get things paid off. You'll be able to prioritize your payments, and then make a solid plan for taking care of every unplanned expense.

List your Goals

On a broader scale, lists can help you figure out your life goals, and what needs to happen for you to get there. While the five-year plan is hardly a new concept, it was my wise father-in-law, David O'Connor, who offered me a clearer way of creating a successful plan in that amount of time. The trick is to create a timeline with your goal at the end, and then work backwards from that point of reference, simplifying the steps one by one until you get to where you are now. Once you've done that, you can figure out what you need to do this week, then this month, then this year, and so on, until your goal is accomplished.

Another way you can map our your life plan is to write down possible steps to get to where you want to go, and conjure up what the possibilities or consequences would be with each action. With all this laid out in front of you, it's then up to you to decide which action seems to be the best choice, with consequences you can live with.

Create a Mind Map

This is my favorite kinds of list. It's the one I use when I'm writing, including the book you are holding in your hand. For this book, I started out with a giant mind map. I wrote down the concept of this book: Organizing your life to reclaim your creativity. Off that idea, I brainstormed every single idea that had to do with this concept. Once I felt like I'd written down everything I could think of, I organized these thoughts into chapters. From there, I did another mind map for each chapter, and then organized each map into an outline of what I wanted to write. With this kind of planning, my writing time has been much more productive, and there's little chance I'll miss anything I hoped to include in this book.

I cannot recommend the use of lists enough, especially if organization does not come naturally to you. Lists will help you to accomplish so much more in your day, they promote efficiency, and it's hard to procrastinate when there's an item on your list that still needs crossing off. If you are trying to create more time and less stress in your day, lists are the way to do it.

CHALLENGE YOURSELF

Baby Step: Create a to-do list for this week, and then break it down by the day. Try to keep your plan light toward the end of the week in case you are unable to finish all the tasks you have planned for the beginning of the week.

Level Up: Along with your to-do list, plan out your dinners for this week, and then create a shopping list with the ingredients you'll need. Don't buy anything you don't put on your list. Need help? Access a month's worth of meals and a corresponding shopping list at crissilangwell.com/free-resources-for-creative-souls.

Be Hardcore: Along with the first two challenges, create your five-year plan. Where do you want to be in five years? You can either work backwards to figure out the steps, or you can map out each step and the consequences you'll face. Once you have a finished five-year plan in place, hang it somewhere prominent so that you can immediately start implementing the journey you've mapped out.

Chapter 10

Cleanliness is Godliness

As I've already mentioned, cleanliness does not come naturally to me. This is the area of my life that I struggle with the most.

Like many of you, I came from a family of collectors. From books to clothes to random papers, I have developed a sense of difficulty when it came to throwing things away. And, as I mentioned in the last chapter, I am also averse to *putting* things away. This is partially because that one extra step can be a nuisance. But mostly, it's because the place I need to put any particular item is so full or disorganized, it can't possibly fit anything else. Because of this, I am prone to piles of my stuff forming hills all around me.

But as disorganized as I tend to be, being in a clean room brings me peace. When I have put all of my clothes away and the top of my dresser is visible, I experience a pleasant feeling of lightness and freedom. When I have completely cleared off my desk to create space to work on, I feel more organized and capable of accomplishing much in my writing. When I have bitten the bullet and donated all of the things I no longer need, even the ones I was holding on to "just in case," I feel like a huge burden has been lifted off of me.

Being in a clean space offers me the same feelings I have when I am on vacation. Everything feels shiny and new, I am free from stress, and I can enjoy life as it comes. When things are in order around me, I feel at order inside.

Yet, I still struggle with cleanliness. Even knowing all of the wonderful things that come from organization, I am susceptible to small piles around me growing into huge boulders of disorder that consume my sanity and extinguish my peace. I have to work hard at not letting my natural tendencies of messiness take over.

As a creative, you're probably in the same boat. Perhaps you've just accepted the fact that this is who you are. You feel like you don't have time for cleaning when there is too much to create. You believe that your messy life is just a metaphor for your uninhibited art. You argue that there is no definitive order to your creative process, so why should there be order around you? You lack quality time for your art, so finding time to keep things neat and tidy doesn't even qualify on your list of things to do. To you, life is messy, and art is messy, so why should your space be any different?

Are any of these your beliefs? Because all of them are mine. At least, they *used* to be mine. And if I'm not careful, these lies become believable once again.

Being an artist does not mean you have to be surrounded by messiness and disorder. Why? Because clutter invites stress and chaos. When disorder takes up your living space, disorder will also invade your mind. It steals your time when things aren't where they're supposed to be. It steals your sanity as your space gets smaller and smaller. Disorder makes you its slave, feeding you lies as it slowly takes over your life.

You may feel like messiness is just a part of being an artist. However, the disorder around you is absorbing much of the energy that should be going into your art.

You are actually more productive if the space around you is in order.

I have found three solutions to combat my messy tendencies, and to keep clutter and disorganization from invading my space. These tips are not difficult at all, but they will require some initial effort on your part. However, once you have set these tips in motion, you will find you have so much more time on your hands, and your mind will be free to focus on your craft.

Keep a Cleaning Schedule

When my husband, Shawn, and I first started dating, I lived on my own with my two young kids in a small apartment. The kids and I were used to the house being untidy, and cleaning was not in our priorities. However, this created quite the dilemma in those early days of courtship. I remember scurrying around whenever I knew Shawn was going to come over, making sure that things were put away so that I wouldn't feel embarrassed by the mess. Rarely did I ever invite people over because it would mean I'd have to clean beforehand. But that wasn't an option for this new man in my life. We wanted to see each other all the time. That meant being in each other's living spaces. That also mean a lot of work for me every single time I knew he was coming over.

What made things worse was the fact that he lived in a very clean space. He had a rule that no one could wear shoes on his carpet. Everything seemed to have its own place. There wasn't even a speck of dirt on any of the surfaces.

Shawn's house was a breath of fresh air. It was also a bit daunting, as there was no way I could ever let him see how messy I really could be.

Of course, time is always a tattletale. My true colors came through, and he loved me anyway. But when we eventually combined houses, we both had to make some compromises. He lightened up on his expectations for tidiness. I learned his method for keeping things manageable in the house—a mandatory cleaning day every Saturday morning.

Oh, I argued against this for the longest time. I mean, give up every single Saturday morning? That's my writing time! And if I'm not writing, that's my lounge-in-bed-until-noon time. This cleaning rule had to be a joke, right?

Wrong.

It took a little while for me to accept this cleaning ritual. However, even from the beginning, I had to admit that it really did make things easier. For one, we only had an hour or so a week when we dug down deep into our cleaning. Because of that hour, the house stayed clean until the next Saturday, with only minor tidying each day. It also ensured that our floors weren't sticky, and that we could invite unexpected visitors in without worry about the state of our home.

The way we worked it out was that one person would take the kitchen, dining room, and living room downstairs, and the other person would take the bedroom and bathroom upstairs, and also do the grocery shopping for the next week. The following Saturday, we would switch. It created an equal amount of work for the both of us, and made the cleaning much more manageable.

Deep cleaning includes the following chores:

- Kitchen and dining room
  - Take apart stove top and wash pieces
  - Clear all items from counters
  - Wipe down all counters and cabinets
  - Organize all of the previous week's mail and miscellaneous papers
  - Clean out microwave and toaster
  - Clear refrigerator of old food and leftovers, and wipe down surfaces

- o Sweep and mop floors
- o Wash windows
- o Clean all other surfaces
- Living room
  - o Dust all surfaces
  - o Pick up all random items and put away
  - o Vacuum couch and floors
  - o Vacuum stairs
- Bathroom
  - o Clear off sink
  - o Wipe down sink and mirrors
  - o Vacuum or wash floor mats
  - o Clean toilet, included the outside and base
  - o Clean floor
  - o Scrub shower and tub, and clear out empty bottles
  - o Take out trash
- Bedroom
  - o Strip bed and put on new sheets
  - o Wash old sheets
  - o Pick up all items from floor and surfaces
  - o Dust all surfaces
  - o Vacuum floor

Now that I've been doing this for years, I highly recommend adopting a weekly cleaning schedule to anyone. It's the easiest way to keep things neat, even if you're naturally messy like I am. Schedule a day each week when cleaning is mandatory. If you live with a significant other or roommates, split up the chores as equally as possible. Rotate the chores so that one person isn't stuck doing the same things every time. If you live alone, you can try knocking out the deep clean in one day, or split it into two days. But try to get your deep clean done in as little amount of time as possible, as the goal is to make cleaning easy, not cumbersome.

Take it One Space at a Time

I think I can speak for the majority of us creatives when I say that we are a messy bunch. Organization is just not our strong suit. Give us an artistic project to conjure up, and we are all over it. But tell us to create order to our work space or sleeping area, and most of us will have no idea where to start. At best, we'll just feel completely over our heads. And if we do manage to clean things up properly, it's inevitable that everything will be back to messy in a very short amount of time.

"Many people struggle with organization due to the lack of skills or having a certain mindset," says Grace Brooke, a professional Organizing and Efficiency Specialist for the past fourteen years with her company, Simplify and Thrive.

"Organized people think differently. It's the way we are wired. However, anyone can learn to be more organized. It just takes consistency and hard work to create these new habits and think differently."

The downfall for those of us who weren't born with the gift of organization is that we tend to look for an easy fix, and then give up when it doesn't work. We'll clean an area of our home, but fail to make things easy to maintain. Or we surface clean an area, but all of the mess is only hiding in random drawers or cabinets. Some of our things end up in random spots around the house, leading to clutter or being lost forever. And when the chaos of our disorganization continues, we give up because it's too hard.

But the hardest part about being organized is when we are faced with the need to get rid of some of our things.

"There is an emotional attachment we have to our belongings," Grace says. "Sometimes that emotion interferes with logic." Giving up things you've worked for, or that have a special memory attached to them can be really hard to part with. The idea of giving it away can feel painful, or even bring on feelings of guilt. The process could take a large amount of your energy or time as you weed through items that hold meaning for you.

However, there comes a point when you will need to make some hard decisions for the sake of reclaiming the space around you.

"It is important to eliminate the unnecessary from our lives so we can just focus on the necessary," Grace advises.

"To create an effective system, we don't want to clutter the system or space up with stuff that is not being enjoyed, loved, or has a purpose."

Basically, you need to look at each item and determine its value in your life. Do not be clouded by your history with this item. Instead, look at your current relationship with this item, and what you project your future with it to be. Are you enjoying this item now? Do you see yourself continuing to enjoy it? Or are you keeping it in a box, hidden away forever? Do you love this item? Do you love looking at it, or using it on a regular basis? Or are you saving it for that off chance that you might use it one day? And does your lifestyle or comfort depend on your ownership of this item?

In simplistic terms, if you were to have lost this item before you started purging, would you even have noticed it was missing?

This goes for trinkets, miscellaneous kitchenware, that old sweater that you no longer wear because it's been worn to death, those sexy heels that give you blisters, that box of mismatched earrings you hope to pair up again, the books on your shelf you know you'll never read, the stack of magazines with fashions that are so last season (three years ago)....

This also includes that file of papers you are keeping on hand—all those manuals for your appliances, your utility bills and credit card statements, that box of Christmas and birthday cards, the countless papers from your child's school, random pamphlets, every piece of art your child ever created...

I know, I know. You never know when you might need these papers, right? And some of these have sentimental value. I get it. But these are also things that are taking up valuable space in your home. Some things, like utility bills, are available online if you need a copy of them. Other things that are much too hard to part with can be scanned into a folder on your computer where it can live forever without cluttering up your space.

Here's your final incentive: you are not allowed to shop for ANYTHING until you have finished purging or sorting the room you are organizing. First, why add more things to a room you are trying to clear up? Second, how can you really know what you need while you are still trying to clear the room of the things you don't need?

Here is Grace Brooke's six-point checklist for organizing each room of your home or workspace:

- Determine the function of a space
- Determine who will be using the space
- Purge the items you no longer need
- Sort the items you keep
- Determine systems needed for the space, and shop for these items
- Organize and add the finishing touches to the space.

Finally, the number one tip to reduce the clutter in your home is to determine the value of something before you make the decision to buy it. If you have no need or use for it, put it back on the shelf.

"The less you shop, the less temptations you have," Grace advises. "The less you buy, the more you save for experiences. The less you have, the less you have to manage…meaning more time to enjoy life and be with loved ones."

Note: My friend, Grace, has a ton of tips on organizing your home and your life, and is really easy to get in touch with. You can find her on Facebook at facebook.com/GraceBrooke. Her website is www.gracebrooke.com. There, you can find her eBook, *Who's Managing Your Life? Creating a Home Based Life Management Center.*

Organize by object

Another way to purge and simplify is to tackle your home by object instead of by room. This is not a quick process. It may even seem like things get worse before they get better. But the outcome has lasting effects that promote permanent organization. In the end, isn't that what we all want so that we can move on with our art?

Here are the types of objects to organize, listed in the order you should organize them:

- Clothes
- Books
- Papers
- Kitchen gadgets
- Miscellaneous items
- Mementos

Let's use clothes as our example for how this method works. First, you gather up every single item of clothes you own and pile them in one place. When I say everything, I mean *every single item of clothing*. Empty out all the closets of your home. Gather the clothes you've packed away in boxes. Grab your out-of-season clothing. Empty your drawers. If you miss anything, that means you don't want it and should just get rid of it. So I suggest you make sure you have gathered up every possible article of clothing you own before you move on to the next step.

Now for the hard part—the decision on whether to keep it or get rid of it.

Marie Kondo shares how to make this process easy in her highly popular book, *The Life-Changing Magic of Tidying Up*. Just like Grace Brooke detailed, Kondo asks you to decide whether you love this item enough to keep it. As Kondo puts it, does this item "spark joy?" However, you can't just look at an item to make this decision. You need to hold it in your hands and gauge what your reaction to it is. Does it spark something inside of you when you hold it? Does this item add something to your life?

Do this with every single item of clothing. If you cannot wear something, don't keep it. Period. Stop taking up room in your closet for items you hope to fit into one day, or that once looked great on you (but no longer do), or that you're keeping out of guilt (that ugly sweater your aunt gave you). In the end, only items that you want to wear and that make you happy should be left to put in your closet and drawers.

Then, you can move on to books, papers, and the rest of the objects in your home, deciding what to purge or keep using the same method as before. End your organization with mementos, as this is the hardest category to purge.

According to Kondo, the entire process should take around six months, which can seem like a daunting amount of time. But if you take this one object at a time, it won't be overwhelming. Plus, you'll be left with a home that only holds the items you love and cherish, and that you actually use.

CHALLENGE YOURSELF

Baby Step: Create a weekly schedule for your cleaning, and then stick to it. Get every member of your household on board by splitting up the chores evenly.

Level Up: Tackle one room of your home using Grace Brooke's six-point method. Be realistic about what you actually need, and what you can live without. Most important, do not shop for any items for this room until you have finished organizing what you already own.

Be Hardcore: Grab a copy of *The Life-Changing Magic of Tidying Up*, by Marie Kondo. At only 204 pages, it's a quick read. But even if you only read the first part of the book, you'll understand the concept of how to organize your belongings and purge the things you really don't need. Once you've grasped this method, start organizing your clothing, and work through the rest of your belongings.

Chapter 11

Healthy Habits Don't Have to be Hard

Now that we've gone through so many different ways to organize your life to make room for your art, I'm about to take away a bit of that precious time. Trust me on this. It will be worth it.

First, let's start with me.

If I had my way, I would spend the majority of my waking hours reading and writing. The end.

Okay, maybe I'd get out a little bit and do something that involves more than my butt in a chair, clacking away at a keyboard. But honestly, I'm happiest when I get to give my writing my undivided attention, or when I get to transport myself to different worlds via a good story.

Unfortunately, this sedentary lifestyle is not so good for my derriere.

When I'm in the middle of writing a book, I tend to spend a good portion of the day sitting at my computer. It doesn't help that my day job is also spent typing away at my desk. This means I am sitting at least ten hours out of the day. Usually, it's *more* than ten hours.

Being active and healthy is something I struggle with, especially when I feel it's in direct competition with churning out another book. I've seen my weight go up and down with each book I've written, I've suffered through the frustration, I've tried every fad diet to the point of obsession, I've succeeded and failed and celebrated and cried real tears.

I know what it's like to be disappointed with weight and body image. And I know how it feels to make a plan, and feel like it's going nowhere.

I know, because I've been there, I'm still there, and the struggle is real.

Everything I'm about to say in this chapter is out of personal experience or through things I've learned from others along the way. **I am not a doctor.** I will not tell you how to lose weight. I will not give you a diet plan. I will not introduce you to any newfangled ways of eating or exercising that will help you drop several sizes in one week. I am not a miracle worker, and I won't claim to be one.

However, I will hold your hand through this. We're in this together, okay?

Before we start, let me begin with this: There are several types of creatives in this world. Some of you have extremely active lifestyles, which is so fortunate for you. This means that you are able to get up and move as part of your art or as part of your daily routine. But most creativity requires sitting or staying in one place. So as I go through this chapter, know that I am directing most of this to the more sedentary creatives, those who lack the time to fit in exercise, and anyone who has trouble making healthy choices in the food they eat. Also, if you are someone who finds joy and fulfillment through a hard workout at the gym, avoids all sugar and processed foods, and doesn't understand how people can gain weight when it's easy to burn calories, I'd like to ask you to be more of a fly on the wall during this conversation.

Let us begin. First order of business is to talk about how much working out sucks, particularly if this is not something you're used to doing. The couch is comfortable. The chair in front of your computer is comfortable. Your bed is comfortable. The stair-climber or aerobics class? Not comfortable.

When working out is not a part of your daily routine, the reasons to NOT workout far outweigh the reasons TO workout. Getting up and moving seems like so much more of an effort. Just the thought of it can seem overwhelming.

Working out is not my favorite things to do at all.

The same goes for eating healthy. It's not so much that eating healthy is terrible. It's just that sometimes it's so inconvenient. You go to the office, and someone has brought a delicious plate of homemade cookies or a box of donuts to share with everyone. You drive home, and every billboard has an image of something that looks delicious and is laden with calories. At the coffee shop, you are greeted by delicious pastries and cake pops. Go out to eat, and only one or two items on the menu are within your diet guidelines, and they're not very interesting, either. Socialize with others, and the calories are being handed out like, well, candy.

And, okay—eating healthy can be so boring.

Plus there's the frustration. You put yourself on an eating and exercise plan to help the scale move back down to where it should be. But the scale moves too slowly, or not at all. Sometimes it even seems to go in the wrong direction. It's hard to find a plan that can be carried out for longer than just a few days. The bad habits you've learned over a lifetime keep getting in the way of the good habits you're trying to instill in your life. The clothes you own are too tight, but to buy something in a larger size means that you accept the weight you've gained. You feel like everyone is looking at you, judging you, ridiculing you, dismissing you—all because you've put on a couple of pounds.

How do I know all of this? Because, like I already said, I know this struggle personally.

Thing is, there are many benefits to being active, eating well, and living a healthy lifestyle, and it doesn't even have to be hard to do. Just a few small changes in your daily routine can change the way you feel as a whole, and can even benefit your art.

First, let's talk about *why* you should move more. It's common knowledge that exercising increases our endorphins and makes us feel happier. But let's really dissect what that means. If you can get your blood pumping through your body faster due to exercise, you are feeding your level of energy. You might think that working out will only make you more tired. But the truth of the matter is, you are adding energy to your day. You will find yourself naturally moving around more when you're not working out, and your midday slumps will start to decrease. This is both beneficial to your day job, and to your art. You will have more energy for your family and friends, and for any extra activities you take on. You may even find a few added benefits to your energy level at, ahem, intimate moments. Wink, wink.

Of course, it's going to take a lot of brain power to get you out and on the move. Your mind is going to give you every single excuse as to why you shouldn't workout. Those excuses are going to be really believable, too. To combat these excuses, you need to arm yourself with the reasons why you *want* to get out. Only you know what those reasons are. But to help you figure them out, here are a few of mine:

- I admire people who are active.
- I feel strong and capable after a workout.
- Working out gets easier with time.
- This is my alone time.
- I can listen to podcasts or a book on tape without interruption.
- I get to see more than these four walls.
- It actually does feel good to get moving.

One of the biggest reasons why exercise is so hard is because your focus is likely on the wrong thing. When you think about exercise, your automatic thought process probably includes things like how bad you're going to feel doing it, how it's going to make you all sweaty, how you'll probably sacrifice so much energy and get so little in return, how you aren't very good at it, how people will think you look stupid…. Did I miss anything?

By focusing on all the bad stuff about exercise, of course exercise seems daunting. Why would anyone exercise if those were the only things that were true about working up a sweat?

The way to fend off those negative feelings about working out is to focus on the positive aspects. Think about the benefits of moving more, like increasing your energy or how you feel once you get past the dread of working out. Focus on the YOU that you want to become—not the impossible to reach, photoshopped you, but the one who is capable of more than you think. Focus on the strong, powerful, motivated you that can accomplish a little more each day that you put yourself out there.

Working out doesn't even need to be difficult. You do not need to run a marathon or spend an hour at a gym. If those are your goals, that's very impressive! But it's not the only way to add movement to your life. Here are a few easy ways to exercise:

- Roller skate
- Ride your bike
- Go for a swim
- Walk the dog
- Take a walk
- Go for a hike
- Join a dance class
- Practice yoga
- Workout in your living room

Do what you enjoy doing. Make it fun! And make it sustainable. If you start out with a hardcore workout at the gym, it's likely you'll end up burnt on exercise after a very short time. But if you ease yourself into it (while still pushing yourself a bit more each day!), working out won't be so daunting.

Don't let your lack of time be a factor, either. If you only have ten minutes to spare in your day, then do ten minutes of squats, or take a ten-minute walk. Anything is better than nothing. And who knows? Just starting with ten minutes may inspire you to find more time to devote to movement each day.

Next on our list to discuss is food. I'm just going to be blunt here. Unhealthy foods are attractive. They are generally super convenient. They're really fun to buy. And often, they're packaged in ways that are hard to resist. Let's face it, foods that are bad for you are really, really sexy. Let's make a list of our favorite examples, shall we?

Pumpkin Spice Lattes. Fresh, delivered pizza. Chinese takeout. A heart-shaped box of truffles. A dozen cupcakes. A cheeseburger with French fries. Ice cream in a waffle cone. A warm loaf of asiago sourdough French bread. A stack of pancakes with butter and syrup.

Mmmmm.... Uh, where were we? Oh yeah.

Let's take a look at classic healthy foods.

A glass of water. Carrot sticks. Salad without dressing. Whole-wheat toast. A small, skinless chicken breast. An apple.

Boring. Eating healthy food is boring.

Or, at least, that's what we've been led to believe.

Your entire life, you have been told that unhealthy foods are delicious and what you want. Companies trying to make millions of dollars off your choices have spent lots of money to make those choices for you. They have done that through some very impressive marketing—things like the billboards you see, the commercials you watch, the cups you drink your coffee out of, the names of the food you buy.... It has all been done to make their product seem more desirable to you, to entice you with their pretty packaging and tempting promises. *You will feel better if you eat this. Your life will be enriched. This overpriced, calorie-laden seasonal drink with a catchy name will bring happiness to your day.*

At the same time that these companies have been vying for your attention, you've also been given the message that eating healthy is unexciting and bland. Your mom wouldn't give you the reward of dessert until you suffered through eating all of your vegetables. Your school friends turned their nose down at the healthy choices in their lunch, and only ate the junk food. Foods like fruit and vegetables don't come in cute packages, but instead are presented completely naked without any flair at all. Plus, healthy food requires much more prep than unhealthy food. It just doesn't have that much going for it.

Except, *it does*.

Your junk food is feeding you lies to keep you from learning the truth. But I'm going to just come out and say it. **Unhealthy food makes you feel like crap.**

It doesn't matter what kind of packaging your junk food comes in. It doesn't matter that it tastes really good. The truth is, you will not be happier eating that food. Oh, it might make you feel joy as you are eating it. But when it's all gone, you will be left with remorse and guilt. It will sap you of all your energy. It will add to your negative feelings. And then what will you do? You will probably feed yourself more junk food in an effort to feel better.

It's all part of the big marketing scheme, remember? You are stuck in a never-ending cycle of eating food that is terrible for you in an effort to feel better, only to feel worse. And then you eat more of this unhealthy food to cheer yourself up. And so on.

Let's break that cycle, shall we?

The first step is to change your focus when it comes to food, much in the same way you changed your focus in regards to exercise. The question to ask yourself is, "How do you feel when you eat food that is healthy for you?"

The answer to that question is actually quite complicated. If you have spent a lifetime eating food that is bad for you, your primary answer to how healthy food makes you feel is HUNGRY. In truth, this isn't hunger you are feeling, but cravings for the food you are used to eating. It takes at least two weeks (in my experience) to overcome those intense cravings for foods you shouldn't be eating, and those cravings will linger just under the surface for quite some time after that. Temptation within those first few weeks is intense. That is why many diets fail in the first two weeks—because it's really hard to let go of a lifetime of habitual eating.

However, once you get past those first two weeks, it becomes easier to notice the difference in how you feel. Eating healthy will leave you full of energy, and you won't suffer through episodes of guilt or sluggishness. Your attitude will likely be more positive, and the foods you should be eating start to taste better to you.

Another thing to pay attention to is which foods trigger snackiness in you. For me, it's anything chocolate or that's salty with a crunch. What that tells me is that I need to limit my exposure to these foods. The best bet is to stay away from them altogether, as I have a hard time saying "no" after I've tasted just a little bit.

And here's a revelation—healthy food doesn't have to be boring! Many recipes out there use whole foods in creative and interesting ways. You can purchase numerous cookbooks that hold delicious, healthy recipes. Or you can do a quick search on the Internet. Of course, Internet searches can bring up all sorts of recipes that may or may not be healthy. Your job is to use your best judgment. Check the ingredients list. If there are lots of vegetables and lean meats in the recipe, it's probably a good one to use. But if the meal is mostly starch and fat, you may want to keep on moving.

Again, this is not a diet book, and I do not have a meal plan for you. But we all know which foods are healthy and which ones we should skip. If you opt for whole, natural foods (like vegetables, meats, and other foods that have not been manipulated from their original form), you'll do just fine.

Finally, never underestimate the power of water. Oftentimes when we feel hungry, we are actually feeling thirsty. If you find yourself craving foods outside of meal times, drink a glass of water instead, and wait it out for at least ten minutes. You may find that your hunger has passed. If not, go ahead and have a small, healthy snack.

Here are a few suggested dos when it comes to food:

- Stock your refrigerator and cabinets with healthy foods.

- Throw away (or give away) any tempting foods that will lure you off of a healthy path.
- Refrain from snacking when you're not actually hungry.
- Plan your meals and focus on what you are eating each time you sit for a meal or snack.
- Keep a list of healthy snack ideas on hand.
- Make vegetables easy to grab on the go by cutting them up before storing them in the refrigerator.
- Bring your own lunches to work.
- Limit the times you eat at restaurants.
- Bring your own food to parties where you know the choices will be unhealthy.
- Focus on how food makes you feel afterwards, and eat what only makes you feel good.
- Strive to make your healthy foods fun and interesting.

Now, let's talk about the "W" word. Changing your focus is not only a good way to change your mind about food and exercise, it will also help you to lose *weight*.

Okay, so I know I said I'm not going to help you learn some new diet so you can lose weight. And I'm keeping my promise. However, changing the way you think about being healthy as a whole will help you naturally lose weight without even trying. When your focus is on how much you weigh and how slow the scale is moving, you will miss all the accomplishments you achieve. By focusing on the negative, you won't even notice the positive.

So first things first, throw away your scale. If you can't bear to part with it, do what I've done—move it into a different room so that you're not tempted to weigh yourself every single day (or in my case, several times a day). Weighing yourself all the time does you no favors. First off, if you aren't yet doing anything to lose weight, why are you checking your weight repeatedly? Second, your weight fluctuates throughout the day, and throughout the week, depending on the time of day, what you have eaten, your hormones, etc. By checking your weight repeatedly, you are doing one of two things—you are either building up your ego or you are making yourself feel bad. And both of these are tied to what you think your worth is, all because of a number on a scale.

So, I'm asking you to stop. Or to at least limit yourself to one weigh-in a week.

Now to change your focus. It should not be on losing weight. If all you are thinking about is how much you want to lose weight, you are going to end up one miserable, overweight artist. Instead, I want you to focus on the benefits of being healthy. Think about how good it will feel to be able to run around and play with your kids. Think about how proud you will feel to learn how to run for ten minutes without stopping, or to be able to ride your bike for long distances without feeling winded. Think about how happy the healthy people you know are, and how happy you will feel by living the same kind of lifestyle. Think about how special it really is to take care of our bodies by treating them kindly with good food and exercise.

Once your eyes have focused on the reasons you want to be healthy, further your success by remaining motivated. The best way to do this is to include a friend in your journey to a healthier lifestyle. Become workout buddies, or be each other's accountability partners. With friends, you can cheer each other on and encourage each other when the going gets tough. You will also have someone beside you who will join you on those early mornings at the gym, sign up for all those crazy 5Ks with you, and remind you of the reasons why you don't need that bowl of ice cream.

Another way to stay focused is to keep a journal on your progress. This can be as simple as jotting down everything you eat so that you can hold yourself accountable. I suggest you also write down every thought, feeling, and success in your journal so that you can measure your journey as you go.

One of my favorite ways to stay motivated is to listen to Podcasts. I'm a fan of the "Half Size Me" podcast (www.halfsizeme.com/category/podcast), a show that features all different kinds of journeys to a healthier lifestyle, and that promotes a positive way to look at changing your approach to food, exercise, and losing weight.

To wrap this section up, you might be wondering why I am discussing healthy habits in a book about creativity. For one, it's easy to fall into the trap of being sedentary as an artist. But as you may have gathered, it goes much further than that. If you struggle with making the healthy choice when it comes to food and exercise, you are likely so burdened, you are unable to be as creative as you want to be. Furthermore, our lifestyle choices directly affect every single part of our lives, including the energy and zest we have for our craft. Your happiness level can influence what you are creating.

Incorporating healthy choices into our daily routine can feel like a struggle, especially when so many other things take up a good portion of our time. However, the benefits are great when you make time for movement and eat foods that make you feel good. You will flourish as an artist, and as a human being.

CHALLENGE YOURSELF

Baby Step: This week, I want you to be accountable by writing down everything you eat. Whether it's a full meal or just a bite, you must write it down. This will not only help you to have a visual of what your daily food intake really is, it will also help you to think twice about what you are eating since you will have to be honest about it. If you

RECLAIM YOUR CREATIVE SOUL

want to take this journaling a step further, include a few notes about how you feel that day. Pay special attention to how the foods you are eating make you feel.

Level Up: Along with journaling your food intake, I want you to schedule in thirty minutes of exercise five times this week. It doesn't matter what this exercise it, it just needs to be some sort of movement for a consecutive thirty minutes. Take a walk around your neighborhood. Do thirty minutes of yoga. Perform stretches in your living room as you watch television. Take the kids ice-skating. Just move.

Be Hardcore: Buddy up with a friend and work together to sustain healthy goals through food and movement. Sit down and create a realistic plan. Then encourage each other in your mutual journey. Working with a friend is the best way to ensure success in anything!

Section 4

Boundaries

Somewhere along the way, many of us lost the tools to have good boundaries to our lives. In an effort to be polite, we've said "yes" to many things we actually should have said "no" to. This section addresses ways to take back the control in your life by treating your art as a priority instead of a hobby, knowing your distractions, and becoming the boss of your life.

Chapter 12

Treating Your Craft as a Non-negotiable

I can't tell you how many times people have asked me how I am able to hold a full-time job, raise a family, volunteer, and attend to every other part of my life, and still have time to write. They want to know how I do it. And yet, when I tell them how, it seems to discourage them even more. Why? Because they're not sure how they can fit their own creative time into their busy schedules.

They aren't willing to make their craft a priority.

I'm not saying this to be mean. I'm saying this because it's a reality. My writing time is one of the non-negotiable parts of my life. Every day I wake up at 5 a.m. and write for two hours straight. It's the best time for me to write since everyone in my house is still asleep and I can guarantee my quiet time. It also ensures that I get a chance to write every single day, since I am doing it first thing in the morning.

However, waking up every morning at 5 a.m. means I sacrifice some of my sleeping time. It forces me to go to bed early every night, or else my morning time isn't as productive as it should be. It also means I have to limit the things I do in the evenings. I rarely ever socialize at night because I'm so tired by the end of the day.

But these are the sacrifices I make so that I can give my writing the attention it deserves. My ultimate goal is that one day I'll be able to consider writing as my full-time job. If I don't make writing a priority now, I'll never be able to make it a priority. So I'm unwilling to negotiate on the time I've set aside for my writing.

When it comes to making time for your craft, can you honestly say you're treating it as non-negotiable? Or are you allowing your comforts, your life, and everyone around you to get in the way of your craft? If you consistently let other things take priority over your craft, you are saying that your creative time is negotiable.

Are you okay with this?

I'm willing to bet that you're not. So then, why would you ever let other things become more important than your art?

Simple. *You don't believe that your art is a priority.*

Before you shut this book in disgust, let me explain. I know that your art is calling out to you. I know that it's consuming your every thought, and that you feel unfulfilled because every other part of your life is taking up the time you want to create. This is the reason that you picked up this book—to learn how to fit art back into your life and feed your soul. I totally get that you want your art to be a priority.

But at some point in your life, you allowed other things to get in the way—things like being a student or an employee, raising a family, being a member of society, and every other part of your life that has carved out a space in your daily schedule. *These aren't bad things.* In fact, they're necessary to life. Nevertheless, they take up a good amount of your time. And as your life fills up with varying duties, you've had to reduce the time you once had for the things you enjoyed doing for fun.

However, here's where the problem lies. You considered your art as one of those "fun" things. I mean, of course you did. Art *is* fun. But in doing so, you put your creative life in the "hobby" category—something you do only as time allows.

As long as you consider art a hobby, you will never find the time to devote to it. And if you aren't serious about your art, those around you can't be serious about it either.

Your art is NOT a hobby. So stop treating it as one.

You need to figure out what your non-negotiables are in your life—the things that are vital to you being YOU. These are the things you feel passionate about, and are willing to go to great lengths to protect. This list could include your family, your faith, and your health.

It should also include your craft.

Now, think about all of the items that are on your list of non-negotiables. I'm willing to bet that when it comes to your family, you have very strict boundaries in place. For example, you probably don't schedule business meetings on the evening of your child's birthday (and if you do, you probably need to re-prioritize your life). If you are a member of a sporting team, you have likely blocked out the dates of your games on your calendar. You show up at work every day at the scheduled time, since you'd be fired if you didn't. At the very least, you have probably made it a priority to eat at certain times during the day.

You have set very clear boundaries around the areas of your life that mean the most to you, or that are required to make your life more comfortable. You need to do the same for your art.

So where can you carve out time to create? You may need to wake up earlier every day. Or maybe you'll have to block out one day a week. Somehow, you need to find time for your craft, and then you need to protect that time.

Now, be warned. Once you have decided that your art is a priority, everything around you is going to try to sabotage your intentions. Friends are going to want your time. Your family won't understand why you're taking time for yourself. Your parents won't take your art as an excuse why you can't attend every family get-together. Those you know and love won't be accustomed to this change of priority you've placed on your craft. It will feel like the world is out to get you as you move things around in favor of your art.

But most of all, your biggest enemy will be yourself.

Many of us were taught to put ourselves last in every situation, so to make art a priority can feel incredibly selfish. First off, this way of thinking aligns itself with believing that art is self-indulgent instead of important. But it also places your art last on your list of priorities. You need to become clear with who you are. You call yourself a mother, a father, an employee, a pet owner, a woman, a man.... You are also AN ARTIST. To be an artist, your life must include your art. *This is non-negotiable.*

Another way you are your worst enemy is when you make yourself a martyr in every other area of your life. You take on too many projects at work. You agree to numerous volunteer opportunities in your child's classroom. You don't know how to say "no" when your friends invite you out. You are considered reliable when cookies need to be made for the bake sale, a friend needs a helping hand to move, your child's classmate needs a babysitter, your boss needs to lighten his workload, your mother needs to vent, your coworker needs a weekend off....

Let's get this clear. Your martyrdom is not you being a good person. It's you lacking good boundaries. If people come to you because they know you'll say "yes," this is a problem. As I've already told you, every time you say "yes" to something, you are saying "no" to something else. Think about this whenever you agree to something. What will you have to say "no" to? Is your "yes" worth it?

Guilt also plays a part in sabotaging any time you've set aside for your craft. The biggest reason why it's hard to say "no" is because you will likely disappoint the other person. If you refuse to volunteer in your child's class, you are depriving the teacher of a pair of helping hands. When you decline an invitation to hang out with your friends, you run the risk of disappointing them. And we all know what it's like to say "no" to our parents. *Augh! The guilt!*

This is where you need to be clear on what your goal is and where you're headed. Is volunteering in your child's classroom going to help you reach your goals with your craft? Probably not. And you may need to sacrifice quality time with your family and friends, but only during the time you've set aside for your art.

Here's something you need to learn to be okay with: *you cannot make everyone around you happy.* This is true for your art, and it's true for life. If you spend your energy trying to please everyone else, you're going to end up miserable. You are ultimately saying that your priorities aren't as important as everyone else's priorities. You are placing the feelings of everyone around you much higher than your own. Besides, if you devote yourself to the happiness of others, your work will never be done. If you'd really like to keep those around you happy, work on your own happiness first. Do you remember those emergency procedures you learn when flying in an airplane? Your job is to secure your own air mask before you assist those around you. The same goes for your happiness. You have to save yourself first before you can save those around you.

Which brings me to the biggest threat to your creative life: your ego. As you place your creative life on the pedestal where it belongs, your ego is going to use all of its tricks to knock it back down, and it's going to use your happiness as a tool.

Are you happy being unsuccessful?

Are you happy spending so much time and money on something that isn't paying off?

Are you happy feeling so insignificant?

Are you happy missing out on the life that everyone else around you gets to enjoy?

Your ego is going to capitalize on all of the difficulties you go through as an artist. It will tempt you with prospects outside of your goal. It will make volunteer opportunities seem enticing because you'll feel important, when all it's doing is feeding your ego.

Very rarely does an artist find success when first starting out. It can take years for anything significant to happen. Along the way, there will be many bumps in the road, difficulties to overcome, and lots of rejection. These all serve as giant blows to the ego. So, of course your ego is going to do everything it can to try and build itself back up.

Your job is to stand strong in the face of adversity, when your ego is trying to steer you in a different direction, and when the forces around you are pulling you away from the path you are on. It's not easy, and may even be a moment-by-moment challenge. But it's vital to keep your eyes on your goal, and keep moving toward that dream.

Here's a recap of four truths to treating your craft as a non-negotiable:

First, protect the time you have set aside for your craft, and insist on that being a priority. Make it a mandatory time in your schedule, and don't let anything get in the way of that time.

Second, be clear on your goal. What do you hope to accomplish? Organize your life to support that goal.

Third, before taking on any new projects, you need to consider what you are going to have to say "no" to. Is it worth it?

Fourth, I need you to become clear on this: YOUR CRAFT IS NOT A HOBBY. It is what feeds your soul. It is a part of your identity. It is vital to your life. The art you create is important. So treat it with the respect it deserves.

CHALLENGE YOURSELF

Baby Step: Make a list of your non-negotiables. Make sure that your art is on that list!

Level Up: Figure out what you need to do to protect the things on your list of non-negotiables. What boundaries do you need to put in place? What things do you need to say "no" to? How do you need to organize your time to ensure that the things that are most important to you get your full attention?

Be Hardcore: If you struggle with boundaries in general, I recommend reading the book, *Boundaries,* by Dr. Henry Cloud and Dr. John Townsend. This is Christian-based book filled with many good nuggets for anyone who has a hard time placing limits on areas of their life, or who struggle with saying "no" to others for varying reasons. It is not a quick read, but it does hold a lot of vital information on taking back the reins to your life.

Chapter 13

Know Your Distractions

Distractions are the bane of my existence. They are all those little things that come knocking at my door just when I am determined to get some serious work done on anything I am writing. These distractions take on many different forms in their efforts to sneak past my barriers.

They are my children carrying packets of papers that need my signature.

They are my dog needing a scratch on his belly.

They come in the form of gorgeous days outside, whether it be beautiful sunshine or glorious, cozy rain.

They arrive as my favorite television show or a friend with an invite to their latest social event.

They show up as an email that needs addressing.

Worst of all, they come as the whole entire Internet, complete with my friends' latest posts on social media and videos of military parents surprising their young kids by coming home (all the feelings! all of them!).

I am a sucker for distractions, especially when they show up during my writing time. It always starts out easy enough. I'll need to research something, so I'll start perusing the Internet for answers. Thirty minutes later, I'll still be lacking answers. However, I will have watched five new Buzzfeed videos I hadn't seen before.

Or, I'll be stuck in a certain section of my writing, and feel the need for some inspiration to shake loose my thoughts and ideas. So I'll reach for my smartphone. Let me tell you, this is never a good idea. All I'll end up doing is checking my email obsessively or scanning all of my social media apps for something more interesting than what I'm writing.

And when the distractions are from outside forces, like my kids or my dog, it's almost impossible to get back into a zone.

However, I *know* my distractions, and you should, too. This is the first step to being able to focus better on your craft—to be able to name the things that distract you from immersing yourself into your art, and then doing everything in your power to distance yourself from these things.

But it goes deeper than that. You should know *why* you're distracted from your craft. Likely, your reasons can fall into one or more of the following five categories.

Distraction #1: Outside forces

Other people (or your pets!) don't understand your need for focus. Most of us are more concerned about our own needs than the needs of others. So when you are working on your project in a public area, you appear available to everyone who enters the room. It doesn't matter if you have your laptop in front of you or your guitar in your lap. To everyone else, you are just messing around, and you have the time to cater to their needs.

Distraction #2: Creative block

You want to create, but can't seem to unlock that key to creativity. Everything that comes to mind seems stupid. Or maybe you're not finding anything worth pursuing creatively. You're grasping at straws and coming away with nothing. The muse has left the building. So you do the only thing you can—search for inspiration outside of yourself. Or, at least, that's what you tell yourself. In actuality, it's just a ruse for entering the world of distraction.

Distraction #3: Avoidance

It doesn't feel good when the ideas aren't coming. In fact, it can be downright painful. You're an artist, the ideas should be flowing from your pores. Your creations should be awe inspiring and mesmerizing to everyone around you. Except, it doesn't always work that way.

Our natural impulse is to avoid anything that causes us pain. When the very thing that is supposed to bring light to our lives ends up bringing us down, it's enticing to avoid it altogether. However, the more we avoid that pain, the harder it is to get back into the groove of our creativity.

Distraction #4: Doubt and fear

These two evildoers go hand in hand when it comes to sabotaging your creativity. Doubt comes creeping in when you least expect it, pointing out the flaws in your creations and shining a spotlight on all your imperfections. Once doubt has successfully weakened your resolve, he invites fear in to completely mess with your head. You'll find yourself afraid of what people will think if you go public with your art. You'll fear that they'll laugh at you, think you're a hack, or totally tear apart the art you've created. You'll fear that they'll discover everything you doubt about yourself, or that everyone will discover new faults in you that you didn't even know existed.

You'll fear failure. And then, you'll fear success.

What if you succeed in your craft? What if people want more from you? What if you can't handle the responsibilities of success? Worse, what if you can, but all your creativity is washed up with this one beautiful work of art or brilliant piece of writing? What if what you are creating is the best thing you ever create, and nothing else can ever compare to it?

Doubt and fear, the ultimate creativity killers. All they need is a crack in the door, and they set about destroying all of your hopes and dreams.

Distraction #5: An untrained mind

Without setting boundaries in place during your creative time, your key distractions have a direct line to you without anything to stand in their way. This is especially true for someone who sits down to create, but hasn't done anything at all to limit the distractions around them. If you don't train your mind to remain focused during the time you've set aside to create, you'll just be wasting your time. What's the point of sacrificing sleep or scheduling alone time if you don't learn how to use it properly?

Distraction is one of the main reasons why it feels so impossible to create time for your art. It's something we all grapple with, and at times, it can feel unavoidable. When distraction is knocking, it's too easy just to answer the door. Thing is, once you submit to distraction, it's hard to bounce back from the damage it causes. It can take a long time to regain your footing with what you're creating. And even when you do push that distraction aside, it's easy to slip back into the clutches of that distraction if you're not careful.

Your job is to fight distraction with everything you have. The only way to do this is to equip yourself with specific tools that will help shield you from the forces that wish to tear you away from your craft. Here are five ways you can stop distractions at the door and remain focused on your craft.

1. Show up every day at the same time to work on your art.

If you are consistent in your art, you are sending a very clear message to yourself and everyone around you—this is YOUR time to create, and nothing else is allowed in during this time. Protect this time. Block it out on your calendar. Lock the door. Make it clear that no one may bother you during this time, and stick to it. If someone needs you for a non-emergency reason during this time, politely tell them that it will have to wait until your time is done.

To be fair, you are going to need a specific end time to your creativity. If it's convenient, you can always go beyond your creative time. But if you have a family who needs you or obligations outside of your craft, it's reassuring for others to know when you are available to them. It also gives you a better chance that they will leave you alone during the time you have set aside for yourself.

2. Come in with a plan.

Once you have a set time, make the most of it. The best way to do this is to come into this time with a plan. If you need to do any research, do it beforehand. Jot down any ideas as they come to you throughout the day, and bring them to the creative time you've set aside. Come armed with an outline. Print out pieces of inspiration. Whatever you do, don't sit down to create without any idea on how to start. This only invites frustration, a creative block, or distraction to come knocking at your door and tear you away from your work.

3. Free your space from distractions.

To be successful in remaining focused, it's important to limit the distractions around you. For me, this means I need to keep my phone away from me during my writing time. I also turn off the Internet on my computer so I'm not tempted to stray from my writing. If I find it hard to escape distractions from those around me, I'll leave the house and write in a coffee shop, or even in the privacy of my own car. Because I am so easily distracted, I know I need to do everything I can to keep temptations out of my reach.

This is why it's important to know your distractions—so that you know what you're up against, and how to guard yourself. Once you know the things that can distract you from your craft, do your best to keep them away from you while you need focus.

4. Give in to the distraction, but with limits.

Sometimes the need for distraction is overwhelming. If this is true for you, it's best not to fight it. However, use the structured reward approach. Promise yourself a good thirty minutes of uninterrupted time, and then reward yourself with ten minutes of enjoying your favorite distraction. With the promise of being able to check your social media, etc. on the horizon, it's easy to immerse yourself in your craft until your time is up. And by setting a time limit on how long you have to mess around, you won't lose the time you've set aside to create.

5. Remember why you're passionate about your craft.

The more you create, the more you open yourself up for doubting why you're doing this in the first place. This is especially true if you've been creating for a while and success still hasn't found you. When fear and doubt start rearing their ugly heads, you need to stop what you're doing and remind yourself *why* you're an artist.

What is it about art that made you want to be a creator? Why does it fill your soul and make you feel complete? Was it the fame and fortune? Was it for success? Probably not.

So what was it?

Write those reasons down. Paste them to your wall. Look at them every single day. Success in art is fleeting. However, the reason you chose to be an artist, a musician, a writer, a photographer, a creator…. That reason is forever. And if you free your mind from dreams of success and money from your art, I'm willing to bet those original reasons are still valid today.

True, it would be nice to be paid for being an artist. Isn't that all of our dreams—to stop having to work so hard and be able to support ourselves on our art? Of course it is. But stop making yourself miserable if success still hasn't come. If it's meant to, it will. I know that's frustrating to hear. But you can't force it along. Worse, any desperation you feel is just going to go into your art. How successful do you think that will be?

Your art deserves your full attention. There are things that only you can create, things that are just waiting for you to conjure up and mold into its true form. If you don't guard yourself against the rest of the world, these creations will never be.

The time you set aside is sacred. It's a gift. It's vital for your art. And it's vital for you.

CHALLENGE YOURSELF

Baby Step: Write down a list of everything that tempts you away from your craft whenever you sit down to create. Vow to avoid these items whenever you are spending time with your craft.

Level Up: Set a specific time to work on your craft, and stick to it every single day this week. Wake up early if you have to, or stay up a little later. The only rule is that you have to utilize this time every single day this week, no exception. The idea behind this is that you're training your mind that when you sit with your craft at this specific time, you are there to create, and nothing else.

Be Hardcore: Re-read the five steps to stop distractions in their tracks. Then practice steps 1, 2, 3, and 5. If distraction is too tempting, you can also practice step 4. Journal how these steps change your ability to focus on your craft.

Chapter 14

Own Your Life

When I was a kid, I couldn't wait to get older. I remember this one time when my grandmother was watching my sister and me while my parents were out. She made us cooked carrots, which I absolutely hated. I told her I wasn't going to eat them, but she had other ideas. We argued back and forth about those carrots, and they just got colder on my plate. I told her that when I grew up, I was never going to eat carrots again. That was all fine and dandy to my grandmother. But as long as I was a kid, I was not going to get up from the table until my carrots were gone.

I was extremely strong willed. Unfortunately, I inherited my strong will from my grandmother. The longer I sat, the clearer it became that I was missing out on everything because of my stance on those carrots. So, finally, I ate the cold, mushy carrots, and I was excused from the table.

As a kid, life just doesn't seem fair. You are constantly told what to do by your parents, grandparents, teachers, and older siblings. *Clean your room. Make your bed. Take out the trash. Walk the dog. Clear the table. Eat your vegetables.* It's no wonder you couldn't wait to grow up. It was comforting to know that one day you wouldn't be a kid anymore and would be able to do whatever you want.

And then you grew up. The mirage of absolute power vanishes, and reality takes its place. You are suddenly aware of consequences to every one of your actions. Sure, you have the power to skip eating vegetables and eat ice cream for dinner instead. But you'll end up gaining a bunch of weight and feeling really unhealthy. You have the power to play all day instead of going to work. But then you'll lose your job and won't have any money to pay for your living expenses. If you don't want to clean your house, you have the power not to. However, no one else is picking up after you anymore, and the house will become unsanitary and disgusting. You have the power to wear whatever you want, spend your money however you like, go wherever you want to go, date whoever you want to date, say whatever you want to say, do whatever you want to do....but you will also have to endure any consequences that come about because of your actions.

So, you may have more power as an adult than you did as a kid. But you have way less protections against the results of your actions.

Isn't growing up fun?

All that said, you are still the boss of your life. You still get to decide what you can and cannot agree to. You just have more knowledge about what will happen as a result of your decisions, and must decide your actions accordingly or suffer the consequences.

And yet, there are so many areas of your life that are trying to gain the upper hand and claim that power for themselves. Worse, you are likely handing them that power without even knowing it.

First, there's your job. Since you have bills to pay, your job is quite important. Ideally, you love what you do to make a living. Unfortunately, that isn't always the case. But regardless of whether you like your job or not, you still have to work to make ends meet.

There will come times in your career when you are asked to extend yourself further than your job description requires of you. Now and then, this isn't such a bad thing. You don't mind staying a little later occasionally just to make sure everything gets done. You're capable of taking on that one extra project. You're happy to share your knowledge to the team to help them get ahead. You are willing to go the extra mile for your job and the good of the company.

Except when that extra mile turns into a half marathon.

Stepping up your game to help more at work is normal. What's not normal is losing your peace of mind because you are giving your all for something that isn't even your passion. Staying late occasionally is one thing, but staying late every night and working through numerous lunch breaks is not okay. It's fine to take on an extra project or two. But if your coworkers and boss are using your desk as their dumping grounds for the things they don't want to do, you are being taken advantage of. And there's a difference between teaching your coworkers something you've learned along the way, and doing the work for them.

I get that these are hard times, and companies are compensating by giving people more tasks instead of hiring more bodies. However, the more you say "yes," the more work will land on your desk. You are one person and can only accomplish so much. Do your job, and do it well. But don't exchange your sanity for mere recognition, especially when you are working for someone else's dream. If you give everything to your job, what will be left of your time or your energy? What will you have left for your craft?

Next, there's your family—specifically the ones who seem to think you owe them. These are the members who absorb your energy whenever you are around them, the ones who make you feel like a little kid all over again, and the ones who won't let you escape any mistake you've ever made. These people haunt you with your past, and don't believe you have a successful future in front of you. They say things to you like, "I'll give you two weeks before you mess this opportunity up," or "Why can't you be more like your sister, the doctor?" or "Haven't you outgrown this silly dream of being a musician yet? When are you going to get a real job?"

These members could be your parents, your grandparents, an overbearing aunt or uncle, or your sibling. They're the people who think they know you best, so they believe they know *what's best for you*. If they had their way, you would follow their advice, but still stay in the same rut you're in today so they could continue to teach you how to live.

Next on your list of power-sappers are the things you feel obligated to do. This is anything that someone asks you to do, especially when it seems like "yes" is supposed to be the only answer. Here are a few examples:

"The art teacher just quit and we have no one to take her place. I hear you're an artist, would you volunteer your time?"

"Hey, you have a big truck, right? I'm moving this Saturday, and I could really use your help."

"My mother is in town and we have no room at our place. Can she take the extra room at your house? She'll be no trouble at all, I promise."

"I know you're busy, but I don't know who else to turn to. Can you talk for a few minutes?" (spoken by someone who isn't known for their short conversations)

"Are you free this weekend?" (With no clue as to what you might need to be free for)

I'm sure you can think of at least a dozen more.

The thing about obligations is that they play on our guilt strings. We will generally say "yes" because saying "no" will disappoint the other person. We don't want to inconvenience them or hurt their feelings. We want to be a good friend. We don't really have a good reason to turn them down. It was our only free moment of the week, however, at least it's not cutting into our other obligations, right?

But aren't YOU an obligation?

I'm going to repeat this one more time: When you say "yes" to something, you are saying "no" to something else. Sometimes we really can help a friend, donate our time, and offer our services to help others in need. It's good to give to others and lend a helping hand. However, if you only know how to say "yes" when someone needs something from you, there's a problem.

Here's the thing—there's a major difference between saying "yes" because you want to say "yes," and saying "yes" because you feel obligated to say "yes." You should always *mean it* when you agree to something. If you feel hesitant, it's okay to say "no." Sure, the other person might be hurt if you say "no." But will your "no" harm them? Likely not.

You are the boss of your life. You own every single thing that happens to you. All of the bad stuff you've endured, those are yours. All the good stuff, those are yours, too. Every single bad decision you've made, you are the one who has had to live with the consequences. And every single good move you've made, you get to reap the rewards.

When someone imposes their beliefs on you, their obligations on you, their ideas for how to live your life on you, and you reluctantly go along with it, you are handing your power over to someone else. You are ultimately making them king or queen over your personal world, and letting them dictate the next steps you take.

But YOU are the born ruler of your life. Not your mom or dad. Not your boss. Not your friends. It's easy for them to tell you how to live your life or steal portions of your time. None of them have to live with the consequences for the actions you take. They aren't the ones who give up their free time when you agree to a longer than usual phone conversation. They aren't the ones who must skip another art session because of overtime at work. They aren't the ones who have to see the disappointment on your kids' faces when you choose something else over them, once again.

Every time you say "yes" to something, you are saying "no" to something else.

It's time to take back the keys to your life. You only get one shot at living the life of your dreams, and you are the one who has the power to make that happen. The longer you allow other people to dictate your moves, the longer you will feel trapped in a life that isn't going anywhere. If you want a change, you need to be the one to make it. You need to be intentional about every move you make. You need to learn how to say "no" when necessary, and stand behind your "no." If you don't wish to do something, don't agree. End of story.

Own your life. It's the only one you have. Don't waste it making everyone else around you happy at the expense of your own happiness.

CHALLENGE YOURSELF

Baby Step: Are there areas of your life where you're saying "yes" when you should be saying "no?" Make a list of the things you feel obligated to do, but would rather take off your plate.

Level Up: Start crossing a few obligations off your list. Resign from a volunteer opportunity you don't enjoy. Make a vow to ponder the consequences before agreeing to any new tasks.

Be Hardcore: In Chapter 9, one of your challenges was to create your 5-year plan. If you haven't done that already, look back at that chapter and map out where you want to be in five years, and the steps you need to take to get there. Next, I want you to take a look at your life right now. How is it lining up with your plan? Are you just treading water in an effort to stay comfortable? Or are you starting to take risks to bring yourself to the next level of your plan? Really study your current actions, and see where you can step things up to help you progress on the path toward your success.

Section 5

Reclaim Your Creative Soul

You've reached the finish line to organizing your full-time life to make room for your craft. You've learned techniques to calm yourself. You've prepared your mind and learned ways to get in touch with your soul. You've created order around your finances, your time, your living space, and your health. You've established boundaries around you and your craft.

Now, it's time to take everything you've learned in the last four sections and utilize them to make your creative time as soul-charging and productive as it can be.

This section shares how to establish the perfect space for creating your art, how to set measurable goals, and how to surround yourself with inspiration so that you can reach your full potential as an artist.

Finally, since you have already done all the hard work to get yourself organized, the next three chapters only have one challenge to help apply what you have learned.

RECLAIM YOUR CREATIVE SOUL

Now, let's get to reclaiming our creative souls!

Chapter 15

Create Your Space

If you don't already have a creative space, now is the time to find it. This place should be somewhere you enjoy being in the house, and have a door so that you can separate yourself from everyone else. It can be a desk in your bedroom or a table in a separate living area. It can be in the basement with the door closed tight. Ideally, it's a place you can claim as your own, and is a space that's easy to access in the time you've set aside for your craft.

For me, my favorite place to write is at the desk my husband built into our bedroom. It's right next to our window so that I can look outside when I'm just not feeling inspired. It has a bookshelf next to me with all of my favorite books to keep me company. There's a place for all my pretty pens and papers. And there's a coaster where I can set my cup of coffee (or my glass of wine!). It's the ideal place where I can guarantee I won't be disturbed, and I can have all my comforts around me. Once I'm in writing mode, I shut the door, turn on some music to set the tone, and retreat into my cave of creativity until my allotted time is up. Life can go on outside that door, and it won't affect me one bit. My dog can bark at every shadow that crosses his path. My kids can watch any annoying TV show they want. My husband can mill around in the kitchen. And me? I am immersed in my writing and oblivious to everything else.

Here are a few steps toward creating your perfect space for creativity.

Find your favorite spot and make it even better.

The place where you are most comfortable is important. This is where you find your muse. It's where your body understands that it's time to get down to business. It's the place where you've always attended to your craft.

Once you've discovered your ideal spot, it's time to make it perfect. The most important thing to do is to free yourself from your favorite distractions. Just as we talked about in Chapter 12, you need to make it clear to those around you, and even to yourself, that this is time that you've set aside for creating. Nothing breaks a creative streak like an unwanted or unexpected interruption. It takes time to drop into the zone of creativity. When your creative time is broken up in segments, you're liable to spend much of that time just trying to get back into the zone. So the more successful you are in creating boundaries around your creative time, the better.

Free your creative space from all interference.

If the Internet is a distraction for you, just as it is for me, I suggest that you make it difficult to access it. Turn your computer on airplane mode so you can't keep turning to it when you're struggling for inspiration. Leave your smartphone out of reach, or even across the room. Turn it off, if you have to. Do whatever you can to ensure that shiny objects, like your Facebook newsfeed, don't hinder the limited time you have for your craft.

Noise pollution can also be an issue if you don't prepare for it in advance. My favorite tool is a pair of noise-cancelling Bose headphones that my husband bought for me one year for Christmas. When I write, I'm easily distracted by any other sound that's around me. It helps to be able to control the sounds in my environment. I have created a specific playlist of songs that I listen to almost every time I sit down to write. It's gotten so that when I hear the songs from this list, my mind instantly goes into writing mode. These songs serve as background noise. I barely even hear them anymore when I'm writing, as I've become so accustomed to hearing them during this time. But they help to drown out any residual noise I'm not expecting so that I can give my writing my full attention.

Music can be a great way to tune out other sounds around you. But sometimes that can be distracting as well (especially if you are trying to create music!). If that's the case, consider adding white noise to your space. It can be as simple as turning on a fan. You can even add a white noise app to your phone. My favorite is an app that's simply called "White Noise," by tmsoft.com. This app has sounds like falling rain, forest sounds, beach waves, windchimes, jungle sounds, flowing water, croaking frogs, and more. You can even combine sounds to create your own favorite white noise.

Adding noise to your environment can also be useful when you have a quiet space to work in. Sometimes silence can feel distracting, or even louder than noise itself. By infusing your space with a noise you can control, you are eliminating one more thing that can distract you from your work.

Keep your creative space sacred.

To make your space enticing to work in, it's important to keep the area free from clutter. Back in Chapter 10, I shared ways you can organize your home so that you aren't overwhelmed by mess and unwanted items. This is especially true for the space where you create. Treat this space with the utmost respect. Do not use this area as a catchall for items that don't have a home. Don't store unused items there, or allow clutter piles to grow in this space. Make it a habit to keep this area tidy and organized. This space of yours is sacred. It's where ideas are born, art is created, books are written, songs are orchestrated, and the muse is discovered. It's where you bring your dreams to fruition, and prepare the pieces of your soul to share with the rest of the world.

This space of yours is holy ground. Protect the sanctity of your space from anything that doesn't reflect its importance.

Fill your creative space with everything you need.

Next, make sure your space is equipped with all the materials you will need for your craft. As a writer, I love having different kinds of pens and pencils within my grasp—the prettier, the better. I don't know what it is, but pretty pens always make me feel more like a writer than anything else. Hand me a great pen, and it's like handing me the world.

Right next to my desk, my bookshelf holds multiple books on writing, and a few that I just love keeping around for inspiration. I also have a large collection of sticky notes and notepads so that I can jot down ideas as they come to me, a large bottle of water, and a photo of my family so I don't forget what they look like when I've retreated to my writing cave.

Your creative space should reflect who you are, and be an enticing place to hang out. You're going to be spending a lot of time here, so make sure it's a place you *want* to be. Surround yourself with things you love and materials you need. Hang up inspirational quotes. Place books by authors you admire within your reach. Add a plant or three. Do whatever you can to make your creative time in this space as inviting as possible.

Retreat to your creative space at least once a day.

It's important to spend time in this space you've set aside for creativity every day, especially when first starting out. This helps to strengthen your creative muscle, and establishes that this space is for focusing on your craft. In Chapter 8, I encouraged you to create a set-in-stone schedule for your art. If you're not already doing this, I urge you to make this a habit. Schedule this time into your calendar, then protect it, just as you would any other important appointment.

Of course, even with the most careful planning to create the space of your dreams, there will be some days when it just doesn't work. While claiming your own space where you do most of your creating is important, sometimes it can feel mundane or uninspiring to stare at the same four walls. If this is true, switch things up by leaving the house. You can easily create art in a coffee shop, in a park, out at the beach, or in your own backyard. Just pay attention to your surroundings, and choose a place that speaks to your creative process without distracting you from your mission.

CHALLENGE YOURSELF

Be Hardcore: Create your own space where you can focus on your craft. How elaborate this space is depends on your living area. At the very least, it needs to be a place where you can separate from the rest of your household, and where you will enjoy working the most. I suggest a simple desk or workspace by a window, if possible, or a room separate from the rest of your household's living space. Keep the area clean and organized, supply it with everything you need, and then use it every single day. Make this space an enjoyable place that is all for you and your craft.

Chapter 16

Create Measurable Goals

You're working on your craft every single day. You've organized your whole life to make this happen. You even have a space set aside in your home just to create.

You can now do one of two things. You can just keep showing up every day, enjoying the fact that you're actually allowing yourself to be a creative person. Or, you can start setting goals to accomplish with your creativity.

Make the second choice.

I know it's freeing to be able to just create simply for the fun of it, even for the release it gives your soul. You're a free spirit, why can't your art be free, too?

Because it will lose meaning.

If you don't give your art a purpose, it will start feeling empty, hollow, even insignificant. The free-spirited art you were creating before will eventually seem pointless, and it will be hard to remember why you were so adamant that your life needed to include creativity. It's time to start setting some measurable goals.

I've been a writer ever since I learned how to form words on paper. But I've been a lover of storytelling even longer than that. The appreciation for a good story started with my mother, who would not only read to my sisters and me from books, but would also weave stories from her imagination. I would curl up in bed while she cast visions of faraway lands and magical happenings, slipping my sisters and me into the story. And, as I told you at the beginning of this book, I would take over as storyteller once she closed the door, long after we were supposed to be asleep.

I discovered how to read at an early age. I remember looking at the milk carton and being able to decipher what the letters sounded like together. All of a sudden, these random letters started to mean something. I was able to sound out the words.

The realization that I could read was incredible. A completely new world opened up to me. I began reading books, starting with a simple tale of *Jack and the Beanstalk*, and then graduating to books that were more complex as reading became easier.

It was in first grade when I wrote my first story. I don't remember much about what the story was about. But I do remember how I felt after I read the story aloud. My teacher praised me for the story, sharing with the class all of the things she enjoyed about my storytelling skills and the adventure I had created. I'm sure she did this for every student. But in the moment, I glowed under her praise.

And I was hooked. I realized how much I loved sharing stories—how I loved writing them, and how wonderful it felt when people enjoyed them. I wanted to continue to make people happy through stories I created.

And so I did. I wrote stories and gave them as gifts to my family. I joined a creative writing class in school and honed in on my craft. I worked at writing whenever I could, and read good books in between.

In my adult life, I realized that what I really wanted to accomplish with my passion for storytelling was to write a book. The question that floored me, however, was this: "What will your book be about?"

I wasn't exactly sure. My aspiration of writing a book seemed like such a lofty dream, I could hardly wrap my mind around it. To think of what it would be about was more than I could fathom. I had a few ideas, but nothing was as concrete as the mere concept of holding a book I had written in my hands.

The passion for writing a book was a start to creating goals with my writing. It's what increased my drive for storytelling, adding another layer to my enthusiasm for this area of my life. But if I had just stopped there, that fire would have eventually burned out.

Your love for creating is not enough. It's a start, but it's not going to continue burning without some sort of fuel to keep it going. Eventually, you're going to need to sit down and create a plan with your art.

Here are a few steps on how to make that happen.

1. Dream big!

Here is where you think about what you want to do with your art. The only limit to this goal is how far you're willing to stretch your imagination. What inspired you to want to create art in the first place? Was it a specific artist? Was it a music album, or a painting? If you've been creating for a while, you probably already have a dream that's connected to your craft. But it likely feels too colossal to think of as a reality. However, anything is possible if you can put your mind to it.

Are you ready to make your dreams come true?

2. Make a plan, then break it up

Back in Chapter 9, I talked about creating lists to manage your day, and mentioned creating your five-year plan. Now it's time to put this plan into action. Take that mammoth dream of yours, and start splitting it up into smaller goals. Let's use publishing a book as an example. As a whole, it's a huge dream. But then you break it up into segments: Writing the first draft; completing the final draft; editing; marketing; pathway to publication.

Once you've broken it into segments, break it down even further. Writing a first draft: Think of a story idea; outline the story as a whole; outline each chapter.

Do this for each segment of your ultimate goal.

3. Give your goal a deadline

Attach a time limit to your goal. Determine when you would like to have your finished product in your hands, and work backwards from there. If writing a book is your goal, give your book an estimated word count, and then set a date when you want to finish your book. Take that word count, and divide it by the number of days between now and the projected date you should complete your first draft. This is your daily word count. If that number is too large, you may need to push your finish date back. If the number is too small, move that date forward. Adjust your end date accordingly.

4. Focus on the small steps instead of the entire picture

How do you eat an elephant? One bite at a time. If you focus on your dream as a whole, it can feel overwhelming and unachievable. However, if you concentrate your efforts on the steps toward that goal, it's suddenly not so impossible. You're still moving toward a huge accomplishment, but you're doing it one mini accomplishment at a time. Plus, it gives you more opportunities to celebrate as you complete each step on the road to the big finish.

5. Daily goals

It's not enough to just show up every day to work on your craft. You need to make that time as effective as you can. The best way to do this is to plan the time you will be using before you show up. At the end of each session you've set aside for your craft, jot down a few notes about where you left off, and where you would like to pick up the next day. That night, look over those notes and map out a game plan for the next day. Then, when you sit down the next day to start creating again, refer to that outline. You'll be able to accomplish so much more with a plan than you would just staring at a blank canvas every single day.

6. Be accountable to your goal

To guarantee your success, you need to be held accountable. The only way to do this is to make your goal public and enlist the help of others to keep going. After all, there's nothing as motivating as having your own personal cheering squad! Enlist a friend to keep you on track. Perhaps you have a friend who needs support in accomplishing his or her own goals. The two of you can check in with each other regularly, sharing your successes and frustrations along the way. You can join a group of like-minded creatives, like a writing club or a meetup group for artists. At the very least, you should make your goal public to everyone you know. If you're very brave, add in the deadline to accomplishing your goal.

All of the steps to this chapter are what I've done in creating this book. As I mentioned in Chapter 9, the section on making lists, I took a huge idea of mine for a book and mapped out everything I hoped to cover within the pages. Then I took those ideas and broke them up into chapters. Next, I mapped out each chapter. I figured out a word count for the book based on the number of chapters I had planned, and then set my deadline accordingly.

My goal was to complete a chapter each day. I managed to accomplish that almost every time I sat down by planning each writing session the night before, and then following my notes the day I was writing. Every writing session, I only focused on the purpose of each chapter instead of focusing on the purpose of the book as a whole.

I also shared what I was doing with those around me. Each time I mention the title of this book to a friend or family member, it becomes more real. It also guarantees I will finish this book, since I now have a group of people who are anticipating its release!

In following these six steps I laid out for you, the rough draft of this book only took one month to write. I never felt overwhelmed or strained during any part of the process. In fact, it felt effortless.

This is what I hope for you, as well—that your dream can be broken down into bitesize pieces, going from something huge and unattainable to something within your grasp.

CHALLENGE YOURSELF

Be Hardcore: Follow the steps I've laid out in this chapter to accomplish a dream of your own. Set a goal. Make a plan for achieving that goal, then break that plan into smaller accomplishments. Set a deadline. Focus on the steps instead of the whole entire goal. Go into each day with a plan of attack. Share your dream with everyone around you. With these steps, your dream will become a reality in no time at all.

Chapter 17

Surround Yourself with Inspiration

Months ago, I found myself in a desperate place. The world was crumbling on top of me, and I could barely breathe. I was miserable at work. I was disgusted with my health. I felt completely uninspired and unable to create. I felt like I was dying, and knew things needed to change. If they didn't, I was liable to quit my job on the spot, run away from my life, and lose everything I had built up through hard work and effort.

I was at my breaking point, and couldn't see my way out of the hole I was in.

On August 27, 2015, something did change. I went on a personal soul retreat, which I shared with you in Chapter 6. I took a day off from everything in my life, and I spent the day on my own, free from all distractions. I traveled across the county, and ended up on a park bench looking out at the ocean, praying I would find a way to control the messy life I had created. I had no answers, only questions. And I spread them all out in front of me and hoped for a response.

I didn't come away disappointed. I was offered solutions to my dilemmas, laid out in ways I could understand and carry out. The idea for this book was born on this day, as well—inspired by the life-changing experience of reconnecting with my Creator and my soul. And one lesson from that day changed everything about how I address life and its challenges.

I was taught to BREATHE and LOOK AROUND.

Wherever you are right now, stop what you're doing and take a look around you. What do you see? Now look even closer. What do you see in the details? Notice the emotions on people's faces. Notice the interactions between others. Notice the colors in the leaves, how the wind moves them as they cling to branches, and the fine lines that make up the design in each leaf. Notice the story behind the smiles and the pain behind the eyes. Pay attention to how people walk, whether it be with confident steps or with cautious movements.

Now, look for the messages in what you see. You could view each action, person, or thing around you exactly as it appears, or you can look a little deeper and find the hidden meaning. WHY do some things stand out to you more than others? WHAT is it you're being shown? Is there something more meaningful about the things in front of you?

Breathe. Look around. Receive the messages that the world is sending to you.

Inspiration surrounds us, and most of the time we're not even aware. Miraculous things are happening every single day, and we take it all for granted. The world around us is growing, thriving, living, dying, breathing, adapting, and creating. The people next to us are mourning, laughing, celebrating, fuming, hoping, hiding, loving, hating, and being. Everything is separate. And everything is connected.

Our job, as artists, is to capture pieces of what we perceive, transform it into something new, then offer it back to the people of this world so that they can see it in a different light.

Our tools are our imagination, our experiences, and our emotions. We also draw from our community and beyond. This is why it's so important for us to not only pay attention to our surroundings, but we should also be with people and in environments that inspire us to go further with our art.

To chase away creative blocks, here are six ways to surround yourself with inspiration.

1. Hang around creative people

While it's tempting to retreat to your cave of creativity and go it alone, we humans are pack animals. We do okay on our own, but we thrive when we have a community. Find other artists you can relate with, and form your own community. If you're not sure how, look up local Meetup groups or clubs that fit with your form of art. Take a community class to hone in on your skills and meet other students trying to do the same.

Once you've found your group, get connected. Find ways to help out in a club, or host a group get-together. Don't just show up. You have to contribute to be a part of it. For me, this was to volunteer as the newsletter editor of my writing club. Before I did that, I didn't know anyone and was on the verge of quitting. But once I started to volunteer, I suddenly felt united with the club. It's allowed me to form deeper relationships with many of the members, and draw from their artistic abilities and wisdom.

A word of caution on volunteering: it's important to remember your boundaries. Offering your services to a cause you believe in is a good thing. But be wary of burnout. Allow for downtime, and definitely make sure you still have time for your craft.

2. Visit places that inspire you

Another way to find inspiration is to visit places of beauty. Go to an art gallery and study the paintings and photographs. Try to imagine what the artist was feeling as they created the art you are now viewing.

Attend a poetry reading, and immerse yourself in the words you hear. Let the words carry you as the poet's voice whispers and shouts, delivers in an almost singing cadence, and places emphasis on certain passages. Search for the hidden meanings, and let the descriptions paint a mental picture.

Put on a pair of headphones and listen to your favorite album, start to finish. Listen with new ears, paying attention to notes you may not have heard before. Hear each verse that's being sung, and capture what the musician is trying to say. Seek out tones that inflict strong reactions within you. Let the music grab you in ways you've never experienced before.

Or go out into the original arena of creativity—nature. Visit the ocean and ponder the waves as they roll in and out. Take a hike into the woods and see the beauty within the trees. Become rejuvenated by the colors around you, allowing the natural world to replenish your energy and stimulate your creative soul. After all, the earth around us inspired everything that we humans have created. So return to the original source of art to find your muse.

3. Step away from your art

There are times when inspiration is nowhere to be found, no matter what you do to conjure it up. Moments like these might be a sign that you need to step away from your art and do something else. You might be too close to the project, or you're spending so much time with it that it feels mundane. When this happens, set your art down for a day or two and focus on something else. Use the time to go see a movie or hang out with friends. Re-read Chapter 11 and find a new way to add activity to your schedule. Go for a hike in the hills or a swim in a lagoon. Take a mini vacation and be a tourist in your own town.

The most important thing you can do during this time away from your art is to just be, and to stop worrying. The muse hasn't left forever. This is only temporary. Take advantage of this time and refuel on life. Your lack of inspiration may just be the best thing that can happen to your creative life.

4. Move outside your comfort zone

Nothing can kickstart your inspiration like leaving the comforts of your ordinary life and doing something that makes you nervous. I'm not talking about anything dangerous or life threatening here. I'm talking about public speaking, having a hard conversation with your boss, telling someone about the book you're writing, singing in front of a crowd, asking someone out on a date, initiating intimacy with your spouse, applying for a job, and saying what you really mean. And for you thrill seekers, yes, you can go bungee jumping or skydiving, if that's what you want. But really, I'm talking about making yourself vulnerable and taking a risk. I'm talking about making your heart beat a little bit faster and doing the thing you've only fantasized about, but never thought you were brave enough to do.

Why does this work? Because it forces you to get out of your head as you try something totally different than what you're used to. Suddenly, you're at the mercy of the moment. It not only gets you to look at things a new way, it will also set the stage for new moments when you put yourself out there.

Try it today. As Eleanor Roosevelt is quoted as saying, "Do one thing every day that scares you." Make today the first day you do this, and watch your life change day by day.

5. Be uninhibited with your art

Do you remember when you were a kid and you used to do things that made no sense at all? Maybe you sang songs in a made-up language, or you created worlds out of colorful playdough.

If being serious about your art isn't working, take a day to NOT be serious about your art. Go back to being a kid and have fun with your art. Do something crazy. Try finger painting, or coloring outside the lines. Try your hand at an artistic medium that's outside your expertise, like learning to play the guitar or writing a poem.

The reason this works is because it's just for you. This "just for fun" art is not meant to be shown to the public, so it takes the pressure off you to be perfect. It also reminds you about *why* you're an artist—because this is something that feeds your soul and gives you an outlet for your emotions.

So let go of the rules. Today, there are none.

6. Take a break from everything

If you're struggling with inspiration, you may just need to put a stop to every part of your life for one day and come

205

back to center. Set down your art, hand off all of your duties, and plan for a day when you can escape from the responsibilities of your life. Enjoy a day of solitude, and just breathe. Notice the world around you without any expectations at all. Be open to inspiration, but don't force the issue.

Consider taking a soul retreat by following the steps I laid out in Chapter 6. To keep connected with your soul, it's a good idea to regularly schedule times when you can be alone and redefine the path you are on. If there are issues that have been plaguing you, plan to focus on these on this day. Find inspiring words that address these issues. Meditate on them. Offer them to the Creator. Then allow the Creator to speak wisdom into your soul.

There will be times when you feel uninspired. However, when inspiration is lacking, it only means you're not paying attention. Inspiration is all around us. You just need to change your view—be it your mindset, or your surroundings. If you find yourself in a rut, this is your cue to make a change. You are stronger than any creative block that gets in your way. If you find that the path toward creativity is obstructed, find a new path and keep going.

CHALLENGE YOURSELF

Be Hardcore: Whenever you find yourself stuck, unable to get out of a rut in your creativity, utilize one of the steps in this chapter. If one doesn't work, move on to the next. You've got this, and you can get through any creative block that comes your way.

How to Apply All This to Your Life

Three years after I released my first book, *A Symphony of Cicadas*, I have published seven books, and have many more still in me. While fame and fortune still elude me, I'm further down the road than I was with that first novel, and I've learned so much about the creative process along the way. I've also been approached by many other artists who wonder how I have time to write when the rest of my life is so busy.

It hasn't been easy. I've definitely had my fair share of setbacks along the way. But I also realize how much I've gained over the past three years. Years ago, it seemed impossible that I could ever write a book. But now, this Mt. Everest of a dream is merely a small hill—mostly because I've prioritized my life around my writing.

My biggest hope for you is that you will take the lessons from this book and apply them to your own creative life. I hope that this book will create the space you need for your craft so that you can accomplish your artistic endeavors, and that it will help you to free your creative soul so that it can grow to its full potential.

Now that you have read this book all the way through, I suggest you keep it on hand and refer to it whenever you feel like something is missing in your creative life. Each section addresses a different way to create order in your life and to make room for your craft. You may have found that some sections were easy to get through, and others took a bit more work. If there was one section that seemed harder than the others, I recommend re-reading that section and applying the challenges to your life.

To help you refer to different sections of this book as you need them, here's a recap of what you've just read.

Section 1: Calming Techniques

Refer to this section when you feel like your life is getting too complicated. If the busy-ness in your life starts to spin out of control, re-read this section to remind yourself of ways to tune out the noise and refocus on your art.

Section 2: Soul Exercises

Sometimes we lose sight of what's important in our lives. If you find yourself traveling down a path you didn't intend to take, this section shares ways to reevaluate your life and connect with the desires of your soul.

Section 3: Organization

If you're frustrated because you lack time for your art, it might be because the rest of your life is lacking order. This section offers ways to organize some of the major things that may be taking up too much space in your mind and routine. Through organizing your life, you will create more time and inspiration to be able to focus on your craft.

Section 4: Boundaries

If you don't know how to say "no," you may have a boundary problem. This section empowers you with ways to take back the reins to your life.

Section 5: Reclaim Your Creative Soul

With your life in order, now is the time to focus on your art. This section offers ways to grasp inspiration and take your craft to a completely new level.

Hopefully, by now, you have a firm grasp on how to incorporate creativity into your daily routine, and have learned vital skills toward organizing your full-time life. You've reached the end of this book. However, this doesn't have to be the end of our time together. If you'd like to stay in touch, sign up for my mailing list at crissilangwell.com/free-resources-for-creative-souls. I regularly offer tips for inspiration and alert readers to books by myself or other artists on creativity. You can also become a member of my community of artists where we regularly inspire and support each other. Join on Facebook at facebook.com/groups/CreativitySupportGroup.

Take care, and start creating!

* * * *

Please take a moment to leave a review for this book.
Your review is the perfect way to say thank you if you enjoyed this book, and I couldn't be more grateful!

Resources

Meditation

New York Insight Meditation Center: How to meditate: www.nyimc.org/how-to-meditate

Psychology Today: 20 Scientific Reasons to Start Meditating Today: www.psychologytoday.com/blog/feeling-it/201309/20-scientific-reasons-start-meditating-today

Finances

Financial Peace University: www.daveramsey.com/fpu

Cleaning

Grace Brooke: gracebrooke.com

The Life-Changing Magic of Tidying Up, by Marie Kondo

Health

Half Size Me podcast: www.halfsizeme.com/category/podcast

Whole 9 Life: whole9life.com

Boundaries

Boundaries, by Dr. Henry Cloud and Dr. John Townsend

Other books and resources

Ordering Your Private World, by Gordon MacDonald

The Good and Beautiful God, by James Bryan Smith

Emotionally Healthy Spirituality, by Peter Scazzero

Acknowledgements

I have many people in my life I want to thank for the creation of this book. First and foremost, I give all thanks to God my Creator. Thank you for instilling me with a passion for writing and creativity, and for guiding me to learn ways to devote my time to writing—even if organization has never been a strong quality for me!

A huge thank you goes to Michelle Wing, Jean Wong, and Grace Brooke. Your contributions to this book are invaluable. I am so grateful you allowed me to include your words and wisdom!

I want to thank Angela Lam and my Legacy and Mentoring Team of New Life Petaluma Church—Jim & Barb Thornton, Max Dreyer, Curtis & Cindy Newsom, Dan & Aileen McNamee, Elise Paulino, Celeste McDonald, and Ann Jones. If it weren't for Legacy, I don't believe the inspiration for this book would have happened. 2015 was an amazing year. I can't wait to see what 2016 brings for us!

I want to thank my husband, Shawn Langwell. You are everything I prayed for, and more. Thank you for all your love and support, and for always believing in me, especially when I don't believe in myself. When I say I'm lucky to have you, that's an understatement. You are my everything.

And to our children, Summer, Lucas, and Andrew. You three are the most amazing kids a mom could ever have. I don't know what I did to deserve you, but you all make being a mom the best job in the world. I love you all.

Books

The Road to Hope

Jill Johnson loses her toddler son to an unexpected accident. Maddie Russo is a teen mother on the run, rejected by her parents and left to fend for herself. Both Jill and Maddie have been handed a life neither was prepared for. But through one shared moment in time, both are about to change the other's life. *The Road to Hope* shares a story of overcoming tragedy and making things new with the pieces of a broken life.

Come Here, Cupcake (Dessert for Dinner, book 1)

Morgan Truly never wanted to come home to Bodega Bay. But when her mother takes a turn for the worse, Morgan packs up her life in Seattle and heads back to her sleepy coastal hometown, taking on a job at the local dessert shop. However, she soon learns there are a few perks to being home. First, there's that rugged sailor who can't seem to get enough of her sweets. And second, no one else can either—because who can resist enchanted desserts? Morgan discovers she has magical abilities that involve her baking. Unfortunately, her magic is the very thing that could take her happiness away.

A Symphony of Cicadas (Forever After, book 1)
Cast into the afterlife, Rachel Ashby is left helpless to witness the remnants of the life she left behind and the undoing of her fiancé in the wake of her death. But the longer she remains close, the more he falls apart. Rachel must make a choice—stay near the man she loves, or let go and move beyond.

Forever Thirteen (Forever After, book 2)
Joey Ashby died with his mother in a car accident when he was only thirteen. Being stuck forever at such an awkward age is bad enough. But when Joey sees the trauma his bullied best friend is facing in life, he knows he needs to step in. However, there's only so much a spirit in the afterlife can do.

Coming in 2016

Loving the Wind
Neverland is seen through the eyes of Tiger Lily, the princess of the Miakoda Tribe. Her people share legends of the boy who flies like the birds, lives with the fairies, and harbors a stolen moon. But Tiger Lily never believed the stories were true until she comes face-to-face with Peter Pan aboard Captain Hook's ship. Worse, the flying thief seems to have stolen her heart.

See all of Crissi Langwell's books at
crissilangwell.com

About the Author

Crissi Langwell lives in Petaluma, California with her husband, their blended family of three teenagers, and a ridiculous teenage dog. She is the author of seven books and a board member of Redwood Writers, a branch of the California Writers Club. When Crissi isn't writing, she's either riding her bike or running five miles every day. Just kidding. She's probably reading a book.

crissilangwell.com

www.ingramcontent.com/pod-product-compliance
Lightning Source LLC
Chambersburg PA
CBHW021051090426
42738CB00006B/287